Marrying Freedom—Uncapping Your Potential for an Abundant Life is a compelling and empowering guide that offers readers a roadmap that skillfully weaves together Hilary Frank's personal insights, biblical wisdom, and real-life examples to show how embracing Jesus as our ultimate source of freedom can revolutionize every aspect of our lives.

- Chuck E. Tate, Author of 41 Will Come

From cover to cover, Hilary's raw and captivating words beg the question, are you ready to trade chains for victory? And if the answer is yes, you mustn't hesitate to read her book. With each chapter, you'll be challenged and equipped to lean into an abundant life in Christ, chain free. *Marrying Freedom* is a timely and timeless message relevant to every stage of life!

- Natalie Reeder, author of Little One Misses His Home and Memory Lane

----

If you're ready to transform your challenges into triumphs and embark on a life of true liberation, look no further than this exceptional book. Hilary Frank offers profound inspiration, invaluable insights, and the necessary tools to ignite a transformative movement within your relationship with a living and active God!

- Robb Holman, author of Lead the Way, All In, and Move the Needle

Marrying Freedom

Hilary offers a valuable roadmap to reclaiming freedom, joy, and fulfillment through her personal experiences and guidance in her new book *Marrying Freedom*. This book will empower you to break free from your burdens and embrace a life of limitless possibilities. This is a must-read for those seeking to unlock their true potential and live abundantly.

- Rob Osborne, Youth Pastor, Zoe, LA

Marrying Freedom

ISBN: 978-1-952840-48-7

UNITED HOUSE Publishing, Waterford, Michigan
info@unitedhousepublishing.com | www.unitedhousepublishing.com

Cover photo: Teresa Williams, Photographs by Teresa; Interior design: Talitha McGuinness, talitha@unitedhousepublishing.com; Cover design: Anna Hilton, annahiltondesigns@gmail.com

Printed in the United States of America; 2024-First Edition
SPECIAL SALES -- Most UNITED HOUSE books are available at special quantity discounts when purchased in bulk by corporations, organizations, and special interest groups. For information, please e-mail orders@unitedhousepublishing.com.

Dedication

To those going through the motions day after day feeling bound, trapped, and hopeless. This one's for you.

Marrying Freedom

MARRYING FREEDOM

Uncapping Your Potential
for an Abundant Life

HILARY FRANK

Contents

Marrying Freedom

Prologue: Locking Ourselves Up

I was sixteen when I had my first run-in with the police.

It was Halloween, exactly seventeen days after I received my driver's license. Nearly everyone from school was planning to attend a big gathering, but I don't think my classmates even bothered to invite me because they knew I'd never step foot at a high school party.

Instead, my friend and I decided we'd hang out that night and be the "good kids." Little did we know, we'd be the ones pulled over, with the police searching my vehicle. I'd be the one calling my parents to come to the police station, while the rest of the group I was driving would be taken home by an officer later that evening.

So what happened in a matter of hours that caused me, the goody two shoes, to become guilty enough to be pulled over?

It started like any other Friday night. We hopped in the car and headed for the four lanes—the main street that ran all the way from the north to the south end of town. It was a popular "activity" for teenagers when I was growing up. We'd drive back and forth all night with our windows down, listening to music, and waving at our friends driving by.

While we were out and about, we ended up seeing three other guys from our class. They, too, skipped the party and decided they'd hang out with us. I'd never spent time with them outside of school, but as far as I knew, they were pretty good kids. They weren't at the party, so that had to be a good sign, right?

Since the Wal-Mart parking lot was at the edge of town and our turnaround point, we decided we'd make a pit stop and go inside. Again, not an uncommon activity on a Friday night.

As we browsed the aisles, the guys decided to make some purchases. After checkout, we should have said our goodbyes, but instead, we all piled in my car. What was in the bags that now sat on the laps of the guys in my backseat? Let's just say it was something in a carton that could be easily tossed out of a window.

I felt the rush of adrenaline as they rolled the windows down to toss eggs at their first victim. We acted as if there'd be no consequences to our actions and considered it all harmless games. We felt so free and untouchable, laughing and joking together. Besides, how much damage could a little egg yolk cause? That was my naive thinking. I had no clue eggs could take the paint off cars. Eggs were hurled by my passengers as I drove around. I don't remember all of the details anymore, but I'm sure they were thrown at just about anything—people we knew, cars, houses—all places they shouldn't have been. Though my recount of some of the night is fuzzy, I can still picture, in vivid detail, the exact moment and spot where I turned my car around and saw a patrol car in my rearview mirror.

I instantly turned down a side street, repeating calming words in my mind and trying to reassure myself nothing was going to happen. However, it wasn't long before I saw the red and blue lights flashing behind me as I pulled up to Prospect Street, one of the busiest streets in that section of town.

I pulled over, and as the officer approached, my heart was leaping out of my chest. I hoped and prayed everyone would keep calm and collected. I felt so ashamed. I knew I'd facilitated some rule-breaking that made a mess of the vehicles and homes of people I didn't even know. Even worse, I was driving with four passengers only two weeks after getting my license. According to the rules of the state, new drivers were only allowed one additional passenger.

I silently gasped as I watched the officer approach in my mirror. It was the familiar face of someone I knew from elementary school. I pleaded with God to alleviate the consequences, even though I didn't feel worthy of being let off the hook. I had never interacted with him, but I hoped he would be a nice officer, one who would give me a warning and send me on my way. Instead, a few moments later, he asked everyone to exit the vehicle.

We exited the vehicle to the side of the road, where there were no trees to hide the shame. I felt so exposed and embarrassed as classmates broke their necks to see what was happening as they drove by. In a small town, I knew we'd be the talk of the town on Monday. All I could do was nervously stand by my vehicle as the officers searched it front, back, and trunk. They weren't leaving any area unturned.

I didn't think things could get any worse, until one of the officers approached our group and asked, "Who do these belong to?"

I squinted to see what he was holding up and quickly wanted to evaporate from sight. One of my passengers had been carrying around brass knuckles, which are illegal in my home state. That wasn't all. They'd also discovered some type of joint.

"They're mine."

If looks could kill, the stare I directed at Mike would have sent him straight to the grave, as he informed the officer the paraphernalia belonged to him. I had NO idea he had stuffed those items into the back of my seat, attempting and failing, to hide them from being found. He didn't anticipate they would search every inch of the car.

"Did you know he had these on him?" Nearly sobbing, I shook my head no.

When the search concluded, the officer again approached. "Get into the car. We're taking you kids home, except you and your friend, since you were the driver and he had a few things he shouldn't have on him. One of your parents needs to come to the police station, so we can talk about what took place tonight."

As I stood on the side of the road, minutes before my curfew, I dialed the familiar number. It rang to the landline beside my parents' bed. When my mom answered, all I could choke out was "Can you come to the police station?" before I started bawling. Instead of driving home to cozy up in my bed and go to sleep, I made my way to the station, with a squad car following behind me. The rest of the group was lucky enough to be dropped off, one by one, by the officers. At that moment, all I wanted was to be one of those people—the free ones.

As I drove my car a few blocks to the station, I felt so angry and afraid. At the beginning of the night, we thought we were being "the good kids." Turns out, being in the wrong company can bring about unpleasant consequences. I might not have known what these guys normally did for fun, but I should have known better from the first mention of eggs. Growing up, I'd been bullied and struggled to find my place. For once, I'd felt I had the opportunity to do something "fun" that wouldn't get me into trouble. Little did I know, something that seemed as innocent as eggs would propel me into a night and week panged with feelings of fear and nervousness. Though I hadn't even touched an egg, I'd be the one to take the brunt of the punishment, if there were to be one.

I sat in a chair in the lobby of the station and could barely hold it together. When my mom arrived, I held my breath, as they shared with her what had happened and the next steps.

I felt as if a weight was lifted off of my shoulders when I heard him say the words, "She's free to go, with just a warning," though, I wasn't off the hook quite yet. "If someone calls in the next few days to report any property damage caused by eggs, we'll have to take action."

I don't think I ate or slept the entire next week. Every day at

Prologue

school, I had a pit in my stomach, thinking either my phone would ring or the police would show up. The scenario, on loop in my mind, was the officers putting me in handcuffs and taking me to a jail cell. Thankfully, and by the grace of God, Halloween was the last time I heard anything from them about that reckless adventure. However, the lessons I learned that night have stayed with me over the years.

Even though it was an extreme thought and unlikely to happen, the thing that scared me the most was imagining myself being handcuffed and having to go through a trial in court to hear my punishment. I would do whatever they wanted to avoid that. My parents could ground me forever, I'd do community service, anything they requested, as long as I could keep my freedom and not ever have to feel any chains around my wrists.

I was desperate for my freedom. All I wanted was to laugh with friends like we were doing just a few hours before the incident, not a care in the world. Wouldn't you be the same? Wouldn't you do whatever you could to walk free without consequences? What many of us don't realize is we are prisoners right now, at this very moment. We've got chains around our wrists and ankles that are triple-bolted. They're personalized shackles. However, these weren't put on because you broke the law. They weren't clasped on your wrists by police officers, as they recited your Miranda Rights and hauled you to the back of a police car. No. These cuffs were gifted to you in the fanciest paper and ribbon you've ever seen. The tag that what was inside offered pleasure, fulfillment, and peace.

You removed the bow, tore off the paper, and opened it up. Its beauty was breathtaking, like nothing you'd ever seen before. As you held these chains, you could feel your heart beating out of your chest. The more you stared at them, the shinier and more beautiful they got! As you put them on, their sparkle and shine resembled that of a starry night sky. They empowered you to feel confident like you were on top of the world, where no one and nothing could touch you.

Alas, the moment passed, and the glory faded. You took them off and noticed a shadow remained. Your skin began to itch, a rash began to form, and what seemed to shine before was now dull.

Turns out, you saw only what you wanted to see. The sparkle you thought you saw was the sun reflecting off the cheap paint and glitter used to cover up the rusty old links.

You noticed a small note at the bottom of the box and began to read. The side effects of putting on these beautiful chains include, but are not limited to, anxiety, depression, fear, loneliness, emptiness, regret, guilt, lust, addiction, heartbreak, and more. The effects are terrifying.

If this little disclaimer hadn't been buried under the tissue paper, crumpled up in the corner, appearing to purposely blend in, would you have put them on? Probably not.

Unfortunately, that's how the Devil works. He doesn't move like a police officer making an arrest in public. He is sly in his ways. He gives us these chains, sometimes without our realization. He moves in the shadows and doesn't want us to walk free. He knows we would make a positive impact on the world around us if we understood and walked in the freedom available to us, so he wants us as far away from it as possible. He wants us just like that little note: buried.

The good news is, we don't have to succumb to him. We can take on the same posture that Jesus did and seize the opportunity to shut down the Devil's attempts: "Jesus turned and said to Peter, "Get behind me, Satan! You are a stumbling block to me; you do not have in mind the concerns of God, but merely human concerns" (Matthew 16:23, NIV).

You see, the Devil isn't thinking of slipping God's best around our necks, whispering His truth and confidence into the center of our souls, no. He's acting as a stumbling block, one that makes us sway, veer, and run away from stepping into the plans the Lord has for us. The Devil desires to be that whisper in your ear, luring you from going in the direction you intended to go, preventing you from moving forward, and running into all God has for you.

There are a variety of ways that he sneaks in, but he always seems to find a way. The Devil places this beautiful box right where you are most vulnerable, right where he knows you're most susceptible to grabbing and opening it.

Feeling lonely? The box he leaves will provide toxic companionship.

Discouraged? A box full of lies, fear, and defeat will appear beside you.

Hungry? Oh, he's got food—the most filling and greasy kind you'll ever find, that's unbeatable in taste.

There isn't anything he isn't well-versed in, and he knows what he needs to do to create scenarios and situations that will distract you and cause you to stumble. Distraction, rerouting, convincing, alluring ... he doesn't just have a GED; he has an MBA in all the tactics.

We can be reassured that, even though we will struggle, there is more to look forward to. We find hope in the promises of the Bible: "I have told you these things, so that in me you may have peace. In this world you will have trouble. But take heart! I have overcome the world" (John 16:33, NIV).

It's inevitable. We will have trouble. We will stumble and fall short. We will become discouraged, disheartened, and feel like complete failures at times. The good news is, though, we were deceived by the Devil with his chains, and we have the power to take them off!

Yes, the chains may itch, bruise, and weigh us down, but they are not permanent. Remember, "If the Spirit of him who raised Jesus from the dead dwells in you, he who raised Christ Jesus from the dead will also give life to your mortal bodies through his Spirit who dwells in you" (Romans 8:11, ESV). Everyone saw Him hanging on the cross. Jesus was dead in the grave. They knew He'd taken His last breath, yet He rose and walked the earth again. That power that raised Him from the dead, that same power, is within you and can be accessed at any time.

If God can raise Jesus from the dead, you can channel that same strength, and the Lord can help you take off the chains holding you down. You can do it, and you will. This is your time to shine. And no, I'm not talking about that cheap painted-glitter shine; I'm talking shining bright—like a lamp on top of a nightstand, like a lighthouse on the shore. You were made for more. You are worthy of more, and you deserve more than a cheap chain that comes with adverse reactions. You were created to be light by the light of the world.

Are you ready to break free? The bond was set and has been paid—it was Jesus on the cross. He paid the debt, so why would you continue living in a chained-up prison? It's time to wake up.

The night before Herod was to bring him to trial, Peter was sleeping between two soldiers, bound with two chains, and sentries stood guard at the entrance. Suddenly an angel of the Lord appeared and a light shone in the cell. He struck Peter on the side and woke him up. "Quick, get up!" he said, and the chains fell off Peter's wrists.
Acts 12:6-7, NIV

No more sleeping, no more chains. This is your angel, your wake-up call.

There is no time to waste. It's urgent, and you must get up now. Quickly! You cannot let these chains weigh you down any longer. You cannot remain inactive, unchanging, and stuck. The longer you wait, the harder it will become.

When I sat in the police station lobby waiting for my mom that Halloween evening so many years ago, I felt desperate.

Prologue

I'd seen the chance to marry myself to the exciting things of this world, an opportunity to fit in, adrenaline, a thrill. At this point, all I wanted was to divorce the disorder I'd created when I was enticed by the promises of the enemy. I was determined to do whatever I needed to regain my freedom.

Do you find yourself in a similar situation? Has the enemy invited you to put on his chains, and now you find yourself married to heartbreak, addiction, anxiety, and a few other things you regret? Will you get desperate with me? Will you view this, not as a trial for punishment, but as one that will set you free? It's not taking place in a stuffy, intimidating courtroom but from the comfort of your favorite spot where you cozy up to read.

Come on this journey with me, where you'll have the opportunity to uncap your pen and sign the divorce papers for yourself. Whether you choose to read this book cover to cover or you bounce around to the chapters most relevant to the seasons of your life, you will be armed with the tools you need. Are you ready to finally break free from the chains once and for all? It's time for you to marry the mighty promises of freedom Jesus bought for you on the cross. Take the first step towards realizing your potential and signing those lines that can lead to an abundant life!

In this book, I pray you find the strength, passion, hope, excitement, and desire to embrace the journey of unleashing your potential. I pray you will transition from distracted to devoted, chained to conquering. I pray you will become stronger in your relationship with Christ and that you embrace the words, ideas, and passions He is placing on your heart. I pray as you step into perhaps unfamiliar and free territory, His blessings will rain down on you, and you will never be the same.

Seeking Approval

Am I now trying to win the approval of human beings, or of God? Or am I trying to please people? If I were still trying to please people, I would not be a servant of Christ.
Galatians 1:10, NIV

Has anyone made you feel inadequate, convincing you that you don't deserve an enjoyable and well-lived life?

Maybe someone treated you in a way that caused you to believe you don't deserve the absolute best and true happiness ... that you are too this or too that for the world around you.

Perhaps it sounded like this:
"You don't have the skills for that."
"You are too nice."
"You are crazy to dream that big because it's never been done. There's no chance you'll be the first to achieve it."
"You'll never make it in that field."
"You don't deserve someone who treats you well. Look at your past and all of the mistakes you've made."

Do you know how many times in my life I've heard the phrase, "You're too nice"? I cannot begin to count. Since when do we live in a generation where it is so uncommon for people to just be kind to others?

I recently asked someone how their day was going, and they prefaced their response with, "Is everything okay?" They thought I was asking because I had bad news to follow up my question.

I once went through a season when someone told me at least once a day I was too nice.

Simple things such as taking a cup of coffee to a coworker,

listening to a friend who needed to be heard, or giving a hug seem to cause the world to stop—you're too nice! Someone approaches you with a thoughtful gesture, but your mind begins to wander and fear is instilled. Is something wrong? What is the bad or undesirable reason for this gesture?

What have we come to expect of others that we are snarky and rude to the people in our lives? It never used to bother me. I love people, and I love showing kindness. That's just who I am.

At first, I shrugged it off. Each time, I'd respond, "There's no such thing as being too nice. If anything, I'm not nice enough." After all, there is always room for improvement. After a couple of months, however, each time I heard that phrase, it started hitting me right in the gut but in a new way.

I became self-conscious, careful of both what I said and did, in fear of being too much. I didn't want this person to be out of my life, so in order to somehow prevent that, I'd just hold back my cares and concerns to make the situation a little more relaxed and comfortable—for them.

Can you relate? Have you ever changed who you are, your words or actions, for someone else, to gain someone's approval and make them feel at ease? Or maybe you are on the other side of it and similar to my friend, feeling like you don't deserve good people in your life?

We pride ourselves on being the generation of acceptance and diversity, yet it's commonplace to see others feeling that they're too this or too that. We feel obligated to change who we are to satisfy the wants, needs, and expectations of other people to gain their approval. In order for them to remain comfortable, we often shrink or magnify ourselves and become something we aren't.

Why must we change who we are to make others feel more at ease? Often we feel that by being ourselves, we're not enough, or in some cases, we're too much, forgetting we were created exactly as intended. Consider this truth, "So God created mankind in his own image, in the image of God he created them; male and female he created them" (Genesis 1:27, NIV). He did not make a single mistake with you. He created you as He planned, in His perfect image. You are perfect. And remember, that's not saying you will never make mistakes or go through challenges, but God doesn't make mistakes with the qualities and passions He gives you. Each characteristic you possess is for a very specific and unique reason.

The friendships or relationships we've had in our lives may have caused us to believe we must meet certain criteria to be "good enough" or to fit a perfect image. Friends may have disrespected you, talked down to you, or made fun of you because you didn't live up to their standards.

If that has been the case for you, I'm so sorry. If that is something you experience on a regular basis, can I suggest this? Perhaps it's time you pursue new friendships. Find a small group at church, or research what recreational groups are in your area. What are you most passionate about? Is there a group with similar interests? If not, think about starting your own and sharing your venture with others! Don't allow yourself to believe you must change in order to fit in. God didn't create you to meander through life feeling as if you can't be your true self. No. Regardless of what you've been through or what others have spoken over you, you deserve respect for being the exact person you are—right where you are.

Are you familiar with what the Scriptures say will bring us human approval?

Therefore let us stop passing judgment on one another. Instead, make up your mind not to put any stumbling block or obstacle in the way of a brother or sister. I am convinced, being fully persuaded in the Lord Jesus, that nothing is unclean in itself. But if anyone regards something as unclean, then for that person it is unclean. If your brother or sister is distressed because of what you

eat, you are no longer acting in love. Do not by your eating destroy someone for whom Christ died. Therefore do not let what you know is good be spoken of as evil. For the kingdom of God is not a matter of eating and drinking, but of righteousness, peace and joy in the Holy Spirit, because anyone who serves Christ in this way is pleasing to God and receives human approval.
Romans 14:13-18, NIV

Did you read it's a matter of fulfilling people's orders or meeting deadlines to gain approval? No. We must serve Christ with righteousness, peace, and joy found in the Holy Spirit.

Imagine the joy you will feel when you are 100% yourself every day! You might not be accustomed to receiving love and support for being your vulnerable and raw self but don't settle for less. Regardless of what you feel you deserve or what others try to convince you of, the person you are is exactly who God created you to be. You were designed with intentionality and purpose.

He's given each and every one of us cares, passions, and desires in our hearts for a reason, and just because they might be off-putting and unheard of to others, doesn't mean they're wrong. It doesn't mean you shouldn't carry out your passions just because it might be uncomfortable for someone around you.

The way I live, the joy I choose to see in any situation, and the peace I experience from God's grace and faithfulness, is not something everyone has in life. I know others don't see life the way I do. I do not want to allow the opinions of others to impact how I live. I want to radiate His peace, love, and grace, and share it with others, even if it seems strange, over-the-top, and unfamiliar to those around me.

If anything, I know the Lord created and carried me through difficult seasons of life to share my testimony of His goodness; He was the one who helped me walk through it step by step. He's the one who's revealed such joy to me that can only be found in Him. He didn't carry me through all of the trials and struggles for me to live ashamed, hurt, and defeated. He doesn't want me to have a hardened heart that lets no one in and feels no emotion at all. He didn't carry me through seasons of painful heartbreak so I could simmer in the suffering. No. He brought me through the tribulations so I could learn how to better love and empathize. He taught me valuable lessons that will resonate with readers and help them break free from the chains in their lives, to live a life of abundant freedom and gratitude.

It can be the same for you, friend. Maybe you're seeking the approval of someone at work, maybe at home. Perhaps it's your boss, your husband, your wife, your children, or your group of friends. You want to be viewed, in their eyes, as the perfect individual for whatever they need. When they look at you or seek your help, you want to have their approval—for them to know they can depend on you, and that without you, they couldn't have done it. You're desperately seeking it, so you strive every day to fulfill those expectations you believe those people have placed on you. They didn't place them there, but you can feel the weight of them. So, you strive, work, and bend until you break, trying to fulfill the "expectations" that weren't ever yours to bear.

It's a draining lifestyle. I know because I used to have those chains wrapped around my wrists like handcuffs. I wanted to have it all together. I wanted to be everything to everyone whose path I crossed. It didn't matter what I had to do or how much or little I slept. I was going to find a way to fit everything I needed into my day, so I could earn the approval of those who needed me, so I could prove people wrong who said I'd never make it.

How'd that work out for me?

Well, I was waking up at 4:30 am, already high-strung before the day began. I'd fire up my computer before I read my devotionals and get to work for a few hours before going into the office. When I wasn't working, I felt guilty because

I believed I needed to be. I won't lie; I didn't even like myself at the time. Every minute of the day was devoted to everything but the things that truly mattered. I wasn't writing, and I wasn't being creative in the avenues I knew the Lord wanted me to be investing in. I wasn't making time for working out, for family, or anything, other than going to work and doing projects for other people on the side. I created a very unhealthy lifestyle that didn't just drain me physically but mentally as well.

Looking back at my journal, I can see I was well aware of what I was doing. I was telling the Lord how I had my priorities way out of whack. I wasn't rested or resting in His peace, and it was because I wasn't making adequate time to spend each day with Jesus. I was seeking the praise and satisfaction from a job well done by those around me rather than pursuing more of the One who'd already done so much for me.

It was this season that taught me I don't need to earn the approval of every single person in my life to "make it" or be successful. I realized I don't have to have it all together or be everything to everyone; I need to be myself and stay true to who I am in the Lord.

After a few long months, I mustered up the courage to take a step back from a majority of my side projects, reevaluated my priorities, and learned to say no without feeling guilty about it. . Saying no does not necessarily mean you will lose the approval of others. It might mean they will respect you even more for being upfront with them, for prioritizing their wants and needs, and for acknowledging you might not be the best person suited to carry out the task.

Sure, it may mean you disappoint some people. It might mean not everyone will be happy with your decision, but that's okay. You are not too flaky, too disorganized, or too selfish because you say no to someone. You are quite the opposite. Peter reminds us in the Bible, "But you are a chosen people, a royal priesthood, a holy nation, God's special possession" (1 Peter 2:9, NIV).

Seeking Approval

You are God's special possession. Read that again! YOU are God's special possession, yet many of us wear the "I'm so busy" hat as our most prized accessory. At what cost do we put this hat on our heads? What is seeking the approval of people at work, our friends and family, and even our followers on social media doing to our lives? It's time to put that hat away in the closet, or better yet, toss it in the trash or use it as a means to start a fire so it's never seen again.

How do you remove this hat for good? It will be different for everyone. For me, it comes through learning—often, the hard way. In the past couple of years, I've dug into the Word and learned what the Lord says of me, what He believes of me, and what He promises for me. I've started to see myself as He does. I've poured my heart into using my gifts and talents to glorify Him, not myself. I've become passionate about doing whatever I can to share His light.

I am who He says I am, not what others think or say of me. When I'm thinking about what someone will say or think as a result of doing a certain task, I remember:

I praise you because I am fearfully and wonderfully made; your works are wonderful, I know that full well.
Psalm 139:14, NIV

For we are God's handiwork, created in Christ Jesus to do good works, which God prepared in advance for us to do.
Ephesians 2:10, NIV

So God created mankind in his own image, in the image of God he created them; male and female he created them.
Genesis 1:27, NIV

"My grace is sufficient for you, for my power is made perfect in weakness." Therefore I will boast all the more gladly about my weaknesses, so that Christ's power may rest on me.
2 Corinthians 12:9, NIV

Marrying Freedom

When I reveled in these promises, grasped how much I mean to Him, and realized how much good He wants for me and my future, my perspective shifted. I went from wanting to seek the approval and affirmation of others to finding rest and peace in who I already was in the Lord.

I no longer wanted to pursue the things I thought others wanted to see me doing. My heart shifted to stepping into the things God was asking of me. Will you do the same? Will you take a look within and see what is driving you? Why are you doing what you're doing each day?

Do you have selfish motives rooted in creating a certain impression amongst your peers? Are you making decisions based on what those actions will get you, be it status, access to a particular social circle, or more money? You see, our motives are what will move us. Can we flip the switches inside of us from seeking approval from others to believing the promise that who we are is already enough?

We don't have to spend all our time serving others to earn His love. We don't have to change who we are to make God love us. We are never too much or not enough for Him. Nothing you and I say or do will ever make Him love us more or less. He loves me just the way I am, and He loves you the same, as you are—broken, disorganized, selfish, busy, addicted, or overcommitted. He loves you so much. You can be affirmed by realizing and understanding He sent His one and only Son to the cross to die for you, because He loves you that much.

Take a few moments to soak in those promises. Shut off your brain for five minutes. Take some deep breaths and reflect on your life. Identify the areas you may have the idol of approval built. Once you become aware, start to pause before proceeding with your decisions in those given areas. Are your actions aligning with what the Bible outlines? When you are about to make a decision, pause and think, Am I doing this to gain the approval of someone else, or Am I doing it because I feel God calling me to it and know it will glorify Him?

When you give yourself space and time before making a move, you become more aware of your intentions. You will have a better understanding of yourself and your motives.

Never forget: The recognition from others will fade, and people will forget, but the Lord's light will always shine on you. Even on days when you feel like you failed the rest of the world, He will still be there. When you step into what God has placed on your heart, nothing will nuke those nudges. If it's in His plans for you, no matter what trials or setbacks you come across, it will come to pass. It might not be easy. It could take a lot of work, but there is no stopping Him. He will be the one constant, standing front and center, cheering you on throughout your race, waving his sign that reads: I'm your #1 fan. Keep your head up. Keep going. I've got great plans for you.

At the end of your life, it will be as if you're up on the stage after a big race, the spotlight on you, the medal around your neck. You're on the podium. He pats you on the back. Well done.

<u>Uncap the Pen:</u>

For some of you, seeking the approval of others may be one of your biggest struggles. For others, it might not be a problem. Some may struggle with it but not even realize it. Take a few minutes to dig deeper into yourself. What tasks do you complete on a regular basis?

____

____

____

Do you find you're always adding something to the list that doesn't need to be on there? Are you carrying out tasks for yourself and what you feel God is calling you to do or for someone around you? Explain your thinking.

____

____

____

If you've discovered you are completing tasks for those around you, why? Are you trying to impress them, to gain recognition or admiration from your peers, or are you trying to portray a certain image to someone by completing these items on your checklist?

____

____

____

What is one thing you can do this week that will help you live less for others and lead you closer to what you know you were created to do?

____

____

____

<u>Sign the Divorce Papers:</u>

"Lord, I thank you for knowing me, seeing me, and loving me exactly as I am. I thank You that I never need to change who I am for You. I know I don't need to perform, excel, or do this or that to win Your approval. I am loved intensely and fiercely. I am Yours, and You are mine. I pray I live my days honoring You through my thoughts, words, and actions. Release me from the worry of winning and seeking the approval of others. I pray You would help me see myself as You do and ask that You help me truly believe in the promises You have said about me. Help me find peace in knowing I am never too much or not enough for You, that I am whole and completely perfect exactly as I am. Guide my steps each and every day, and let my life be a reflection of You to those around me."

Overcoming Rejection

We are hard pressed on every side, but not crushed;
perplexed, but not in despair; persecuted, but not
abandoned; struck down, but not destroyed.
2 Corinthians 4:8-9, NIV

You didn't get selected for the job. They picked someone else for the part. Your colleague received the promotion. He or she didn't want to be a part of your life any longer.

I think all of us can agree to experience any of those things hurts.

When you ask for something, it's with the hope and intention of hearing yes to whatever you're seeking. When you care about someone, you have the hope that the feeling is mutual. However, that is not always the case—you won't always hear yes, and you won't always have a say in what happens in your life. We all face rejection at some point. Whether it's in your career, relationships, or dreams, rejection can prompt feelings of defeat and discouragement that cause you to question yourself.

Why am I not good enough?
Why is that person better than me?
Why am I not worthy of your love?
Why is she so bitter towards me without reason?
Why? Why? Why?

The questions and doubts that rejection can root in your heart can be detrimental to your confidence and self-esteem. It can be heartbreaking. It can cause tremendous pain and anguish, leaving you feeling paralyzed and hopeless.

The Frustrating Job Hunt

How many times have you been rejected for a job you really wanted? I can't count the number of times I've received a call or an email informing me I hadn't been picked for a position.

When I first started applying for jobs after college, each no I received was a blow to my self-confidence. Negative thoughts began creeping in, but I still sought the place the Lord was guiding me, even though I was feeling lost and uncertain about where He was leading.

I didn't have any idea what I even wanted to do but knew that God had a plan, and I was eager to pursue it. I knew it would all work out for good. However, what started out as an exciting and wonder-filled job hunt, shifted into a doubt-filled and anxiety-ridden season. My confidence walked right out the door, along with my hope and determination.

I don't have the experience they're listing in their "requirements," so why apply?

There's probably someone out there who's more skilled than me in these areas.

I know I'm lacking one of the qualifications listed, so I won't get it. I'm not even going to submit an application. It's a waste of time.

There were many tears and feelings of disappointment that came along with a fresh rejection email or call. No meant I had to continue the hunt. It meant more hours on my laptop submitting resumes and cover letters, hoping and praying that this time, it wouldn't be a waste.

As time went on and I continued to pray and seek where the Lord wanted me, I embraced the promise, "And my God will meet all your needs according to the riches of his glory in Christ Jesus" (Philippians 4:19, NIV). I felt my perspective shift. Rather than feeling discouraged when I received a rejection, I rejoiced. Each no I received meant I was one no closer to the best yes that He had for me. He would meet my needs, and He wouldn't let me down. While it wasn't easy, particularly when I was turned down for a job I would have enjoyed doing, I knew it wasn't the perfect fit for me, so I had to keep on persevering. He taught me to keep my eyes on Jesus and trust Him to lead me to it in His timing, not mine.

The absolute truth is, He won't keep any good thing from us—not from you, not from me. He will protect us from those things that will distract us or lead us away from the path He is creating for us. The jobs I'd been applying to weren't fit for me, and I wasn't fit for them.

One job wouldn't have allowed me to use the gifts and talents the Lord has blessed me with in the way He wanted me to. The other, He knew if He gave me that role right now, I wouldn't be ready. I would be crushed under the weight of the blessing, because I wouldn't have the adequate and necessary time to prepare for what He had planned.

Rather than allowing the plans to work out within a week or two, He was teaching me patience, giving me discernment and clarity, and allowing me to discover new passions I hadn't taken the time to realize.

There came a point when I thought for certain I was getting a job. I knew I'd aced the interviews, the conversations clicked and flowed with the two colleagues I'd be working with, and when I toured the office space, I felt an overwhelming sense of this is where I'm supposed to be.

Days later, I got the call. They had picked someone else.

At that time, I had been walking through a series of no's, and those hadn't bothered me. In all honesty, I had been putting in applications to countless job openings for the purpose of being able to answer, "Yeah, I've been applying to this company or that," if someone were to ask. I wasn't doing it because it was something I wanted, but more so, to create an image for others. I didn't feel any sort of attachment to the outcome. However, with this position, I'd gotten my hopes up and was excited and expectant about the possibility. With that rejection came extreme feelings of discouragement. I'd thought it was the one. Now, I'd have to start all over, yet again.

I was driving through a parking lot to visit my sister-in-law at work when the song, "Words I Would Say," by Sidewalk Prophets came on. The song is one that spoke to me after a friend passed away unexpectedly a few years earlier. When it came on, it was as if my friend were still here, reassuring me I needed to remain strong in the Lord.

Tears began to stream down my face as I parked my car, took a deep breath, and regained my composure. I needed to refocus and remain steadfast in the truth that He was working it out. I just needed to keep my eyes on Him—on what He was doing and not so much on what I thought I needed to be doing. He had it all under control; it was going to be fine. It was going to be better than I could even imagine. Yes, this rejection stung, but I knew pursuing things in my own strength would sting even more. I was going to do great things; I just needed to wait a little longer.

Later on that tear-jerking Monday, I went to Bible study and discussed the difficulty of finding a job with one of the gals there. She mentioned she knew of someone looking for help with their marketing at a local gym. She gave me his contact information, and I sent off my resume the next day. A few days later, we had a phone conversation, and the following Monday, I went in to meet with him. Tuesday was my first day of employment there. All of this happened within a matter of eight days. I met a man there who first became my personal trainer, then grew into my best friend, and is now my husband and biggest encourager.

Did God have ironic timing and plans or what?

He knew I'd be upset and frustrated with the process, but He knew He had something better in store for me. It all fell into place, just as He knew it would.

For each no, I am grateful. For each rejection I faced, I thank the Lord for protecting me. He taught me to give myself grace when I wanted to give up. He gave me a schedule that allowed slower-paced mornings, where I could dig deeper and learn more from the Word of God. He allowed rejection, because He knew I wasn't ready for the promise. Instead, He granted me a season of preparation. It gave me time to devote to discovering and developing my passions and skills. He knew I needed that season of sharpening in order to help set others free.

When you face rejection, it's not because God doesn't care about you or doesn't want you to be happy. He knows your struggles, and He knows your heart. He is using the time to prepare you for His best yes, even if the process doesn't seem as simple. The delay and rejection are for our ultimate good, as He promises, "And we know that in all things God works for the good of those who love him, who have been called according to his purpose" (Romans 8:28, NIV).

Do you want to know something else that was ironic about that whole situation? Those I'd interviewed with previously had wanted to grab coffee a few months later to see how I was doing. They wanted to maintain a connection because, though they didn't hire me for that position, they wanted to stay in touch for future opportunities. We chatted, and the subject came up that I was considering moving closer to Peoria, the city where I was working, so I wouldn't have to commute two hours each day.

They said they had a gal that worked for them who would be the perfect roommate for me and they'd connect us via email. I might not have gotten the job there, but today, as I write this, she is one of my best friends. She is the sweetest, most bubbly, and God-fearing woman I know. We've laughed and dreamed big together, and I've watched her take chances and trust the Lord with her God-sized dreams. It's been the most amazing thing to watch her leave her full-time job to pursue her photography business and to see how the Lord has honored her faithfulness in that decision. By looking at her, you see she radiates such joy and light, something I attribute to a life lived with Jesus. And, a fun fact, she is the one who took the photo for the cover of this book. Talk about a talented best friend. Thank you, Jesus, for working in ways we can never understand.

Don't lose heart. There's beauty wrapped up in each no you receive. It might be different than you would have ever anticipated, but it's good, so so good.

Rejection in Close Relationships

Okay, so maybe you're thinking, *Well, that's all good and sounds great, but my rejection hasn't come in the form of a job hunt. No. Mine has been much more personal. It came in the form of a personal relationship, someone in my family, or a close friend. They turned and walked away, rejecting me, at a time I didn't expect. What about that, Hil? That hurts a lot more than being turned down for a job.*

I feel you. I know it hurts. I know the pain can seem unbearable at times. I know you want to throw your hands up in the air and get rid of the pain and hurt that come with it. You didn't ask for it, but somehow, it is yours to deal with. Rejected. Feeling alone and abandoned. The pain cuts deep. I know because I've felt it, and I want to wrap my arms around you right now if you are feeling it. You don't deserve it, and I am so sorry you are walking through this. But friend, I promise you there is strength in Jesus. I can promise you because He was my strength in the times when I was at my lowest.

It can be difficult to put one foot in front of the other when the pain clouds your vision. The rejection creates blows in your confidence. It shuns the security we find in Jesus' promises of hope and love.

We tend to forget His great love for us when we're feeling so rejected by someone, when we're walking through the valley. We must somehow muster the strength to refocus our eyes on Him and remember what He doesn't allow to happen is with good reason, and what He takes away might not make sense now, but it is for our good. Yes, it stinks. Yes, it hurts. I know; you're tired of waiting. No one wants to go through it, BUT the Lord doesn't want you to settle when He has someone amazing He created just for you—a friendship, a relationship, or a marriage-that will launch you into your destiny rather than the friendship you had your eye on. It would have distracted you from the path He created you to walk.

Consider Joseph's story. His own family members rejected him. In Genesis 37, Joseph's brothers planned to kill him because they were jealous of him. They had the idea to throw him in a pit and tell everyone that an animal ate him. They ended up sparing his life and selling him into slavery. While he was a slave, "Joseph's master took him and put him in prison, the place where the king's prisoners were confined" (Genesis 39:20, NIV).

Do you know who was there with him, the entire time, and never once rejected him, through all of the challenges? The Lord! He did the opposite. God "showed him kindness and granted him favor in the eyes of the prison warden" (Genesis 39:21, NIV). Joseph may have been rejected, but God was using his rejection as His tool to shape Joseph to impact others.

Sometimes, it seems hard to imagine the Lord is elevating you when you are walking through difficult seasons. Imagine trying to see good when you're chained to prison walls like Joseph. But God was faithful, and His plan prevailed. After a turn of events, Joseph was chosen to interpret dreams for Pharaoh, and then, he was selected as prime minister, progressing from pit to prince. He helped prepare the land for the coming famine.

His brothers ventured to Egypt from Canaan for grain, seeking Joseph without realizing it was their brother. Joseph sent his attendants out of the room and broke the news to them:

*Then Joseph said to his brothers, "Come close to me."
When they had done so, he said, "I am your brother
Joseph, the one you sold into Egypt! And now, do not be
distressed and do not be angry with yourselves for selling
me here, because it was to save lives that God sent me
ahead of you. For two years now there has been famine
in the land, and for the next five years there will be no
plowing and reaping. But God sent me ahead of you to
preserve for you a remnant on earth and to save your lives
by a great deliverance.*
Genesis 45:4-7, NIV

Was he mad at them when he saw them? No. It continues, "Then he threw his arms around his brother Benjamin and wept, and Benjamin embraced him, weeping. And he kissed all his brothers and wept over them. Afterward his brothers talked with him" (Genesis 45:14-15, NIV).

Sure, some of our stories might not look like restoration, as was the case for Joseph, but God can still move in the background as He did here.

If I'm honest with you, this is one of the most challenging topics for me to share. Unlike in this passage, my rejection didn't resolve the way I envisioned it. It didn't end in resolution and a restored relationship, as it did at the end of Joseph's story when he was able to reunite with his brothers and father and save them from the famine. In my story, there was never an, "I'm sorry for the way things have been. I forgive you."

The hardest part is, this rejection stemmed from a web of lies, which I had no idea about until it was too late.

I noticed it for the first time at a family event. I went to talk with this family member, and she would barely look me in the eye. I was surprised and confused, to say the least. A few days later, word in our small-town neighborhood was that this person was letting all of our neighbors know that I had stolen from her. Well, I guess that explained why she wouldn't look at me. But, shock was what I felt. Hurt. Disbelief. Confusion.

Overcoming Rejection

Where did this come from?

I went over to visit with her, to try to get some clarity about the situation and to clear the air. When I brought up the rumors I heard, she wanted nothing to do with it. She didn't believe a word I said and reiterated, "You stole from me. You took my sweaters, and you put a $100 bill on my Bible. I know it was you."

Have you ever felt helpless in a situation because you couldn't control it? The other person had already made up their mind and would not change it, no matter what? That's how I felt. She wasn't budging, and to be honest, for a year and a half after that, we didn't see each other. We lived less than two minutes away from one another. The holidays came and went, birthdays passed, and not a single call, visit, nothing. My brother still received his birthday cards, but me? Nothing. I covered it up just fine, but can I tell you, it stung, just like the sting when I sliced my finger washing a canning lid in the dishes and had to put peroxide on it.

Time has taught me much about life, and if I were the person I am now when this all began, I know I would have had the courage to go over there again. I wouldn't have let it persist. I would have gone and set things straight. Instead of running for fear of rejection, I would have run into reparation. For a year and a half, each time I passed the house, I wanted things to be different. For months after it occurred, she would tell her friends and people around our neighborhood about what "I'd done." Each of them would pass it along to me, and each and every time, it felt like a dagger to the heart.

But even as time taught me more boldness and confidence in the Lord, which I lacked at the time, I didn't go to her house and I didn't try to mend it. After the conversation we'd had, where she wasn't changing her mind, I let that determine how the next year and a half went. I let the pain paralyze me. I let the rejection and the accusation tie chains around my entire body. I was chained down, just like Joseph when he wound up in prison.

Marrying Freedom

I remember one Friday, after work, she was in the hospital in the town where I now live, and I decided I was going to go see her. It'd been a year and a half since I'd been in the same room or talked with her. God kept placing it on my heart to go there. I wanted to tell Him, "Nope, no way, Lord." I didn't want to muster up the strength and courage to do it. I didn't want her to look at me the way she had the last time I saw her, with such hateful and unforgiving eyes. However, the hours passed and the weight of needing to go to the hospital kept growing. After work, I stopped at Walgreens and picked up a puzzle book and some fuzzy socks for her, since it was the middle of winter. I drove to the hospital, praying with each passing mile, because I needed every ounce of courage God could give me.

As the doors closed on the elevator to take me to her floor, I felt like I was going to pass out. My heart was pounding, and I was as anxious as ever. When I walked into her room, there were doctors and someone was lying in the bed, but as I looked closer, I realized it wasn't her. Confused, I went to the nurses' station and asked if I had the wrong room. She was supposed to be in there until Saturday, but turns out, she had just been released a few hours earlier. I felt foolish and sad and overcome with emotion. Yet, I knew the Lord had shown me that it was possible to take that scary step with Him; He wasn't leaving me.

Two days later, at church, the sermon was about forgiveness. The pastor ended it with a challenge, to reach out to the person who was in our heart. I was getting the impression the Lord wasn't going to let me sit back idly any longer.

That afternoon, I sat on the back porch, and hands shaking, I dialed her number. She picked up, and we small-talked for a few minutes. She acted as if nothing had happened; as if it hadn't been so long since we last spoke. I am not one for letting things go and acting like they never happened, especially something like this. When the conversation shifted, I knew it was time.

I apologized. I told her how sorry I was for the way things had turned out and how they had been. I thought this was it—this would be our moment to rekindle the relationship and go back to some sort of communication. God had shown me two opportunities within two days, so surely He would be in this—He would fill it with grace and forgiveness.

But ... my words were not welcome; I was not shown grace. They were not returned with mercy or an apology on her end.

"You should not have done what you did."

I calmly replied, "Can you please explain to me what I did?"

"You stole from me, and you never should have done that."

Well ... I tried. God knew the truth. I knew He was aware of the back story, and the heart behind the person who had planted these lies in her mind time and time again. I was certain He had heard my prayers and that He already knew how this conversation would go. Before I even made the call, He felt my pain that would result from dialing her number. He was there, drawing me close when I cried my eyes out over something that didn't and wasn't going to change.

I don't have a pretty, promising end of this story to share with you, because that's not what happened. We talked a few times after that. I was able to call and share the news of my engagement. A few months later, her health was declining and COVID hit, so there was no visiting, even if I'd wanted to. We went as a family to visit through the window one day and spoke with her on the phone while we stood outside. It was the first time I had seen her in two years.

Within a week, she was gone. There was no miraculous restoration before she passed. I couldn't even express what my heart was feeling. Still, to this day, there are moments when I'm just overcome with the emotion of it.

It hasn't been easy. There have been periods of time where I blame myself, asking, what's wrong with me, and why would someone ever believe something so untrue, as in this case? I questioned what I could have done differently and what I ever did to make her believe this. Why wasn't I braver; why didn't I confront the situation head-on and clear the air right when it happened? Why did I let fear and pain control my life, allowing the devil to steal my last two years with her?

I can't make it make sense. It never did, and I know, one day in heaven, it will. For now, I rest in Jesus' promises. I find strength and grace in knowing, "The thief comes only to steal and kill and destroy; I have come that they may have life, and have it to the full" (John 10:10, NIV). I know He will restore, in abundance, what has been taken and lacking. I know He will provide for me and fill the voids until my heart is overflowing, as He will do for you.

No, it doesn't make sense, but I still have full confidence that the Lord is working behind the scenes, and even if I don't understand His plan for this situation on this side of Heaven, He is still in it.

There have been many moments of deep doubting, and that's when I have to pause and reflect on what God has done and how faithful He has been. I must remember how full my cup has felt on so many occasions after time spent with family and friends. I remind myself I can't get stuck in the wishing and the what-ifs. I might not have the one relationship I longed to have restored, but He continues to weave others into my story. Maybe they are different relationships than I ever pictured or imagined for my life, but they have been beautiful.

I don't want you to read this and lose all hope, and I also don't want you to think it's going to turn out the same for you. Though the ending to this story doesn't seem happy, there's still such beauty that has come from it, even if it looks different than I desired. He's shown me His love, taught me to trust in Him with every ounce of my being, and challenged me to find wholeness in Him and His plan rather than my plans for how I want things to be. He might take away someone you, with every ounce of your strength, wanted in your life, but remember how faithful He has been, and that from the ashes, He can create masterpieces.

What I've learned through the many facets of rejection is this: what I thought I "needed" at the time, what I thought was so "good" for me, was not. As a matter of fact, it was just a stepping stone in preparation for what He had in store.

Maybe you thought applying to that job was exactly what He had in mind, but you came to find out there was an even better fit for you; one that allowed you to use your God-given talents 90% of the time, rather than the 50% at the other place.

Maybe a friendship, relationship, or family member rejected you and didn't want you in their life; that doesn't mean there is something wrong with you or that you don't deserve the relationship your heart longs for. Jesus can fill that void in such sweeter ways. Yes, it might hurt a lot, and you might question why, but Jesus will show you His heart. He will love you, regardless of how unloved you feel.

He will not take away something without reason. He will not prevent you from landing that "perfect" job. He will not take away your "perfect" future spouse. He will not allow rejection without the perfect reasoning for it.

I'll close with this. Rejection hurts, but what if next time you're experiencing it, you look at it through the lens that sees protection rather than rejection? He's protecting you from the things that wouldn't be best for you, preparing you for what's to come. In the meantime, He is your Healer, Provider, and Guide through your circumstances so you can find peace, hope, and healing, and that's a reason for celebration.

Uncap the Pen:

Take a few minutes to jot down any rejections you are facing or have faced in the past.

____

____

____

How did you react to these rejections? Has it caused you to question yourself and your abilities? Did you see it as the Lord directing you to something even better? Write your thoughts out here.

____

____

____

Whether this rejection is something brand new or it happened months or years ago, did you see something good come out of it? Try to look at it from that perspective, and see what good you can discern from that circumstance.

____

____

____

Next time you are faced with rejection, what is one thing you want to remember when walking through it?

____

____

<u>Sign the Divorce Papers:</u>

"Lord, give me the strength to let go of anything that stands contrary to Your will for me. Help me stay focused on the truth of what You say about me, regardless of any rejection I face. Let Your Word saturate my mind, and help me know that whatever or whoever You are protecting me from is for Your glory, for my good, and the best path for me. May I cling to Your Word, Your love, Your wholeness, and Your peace above all else. Give me the direction, guidance, discernment, and courage to face opposition with grace and boldness, so I may walk confidently in the path You've created for me to walk. In Jesus' name."

Healing After a Heartbreak

Come to me all you who are weary and burdened, and
I will give you rest.
Matthew 11:28, NIV

Heartbreak can be one of the hardest seasons to walk through. Pain from losing a romantic partner, a friend, or a family member is always difficult to handle. Or maybe, it has nothing at all to do with a person. Perhaps it's the loss of a job or possession, a decline in health, or the passing of a pet. Heartbreak is a hurdle that hinders a myriad of hearts.

It's one thing to see it coming, to have a general idea that things aren't going well. You know there's a chance you might lose it. There's strain, tension, and a string of problems arising between parties. There are problems at work. The pet is sick and fragile. However, when you don't see it coming and you are blindsided by the unexpected, things can feel impossible to navigate.

There is someone in the Bible who can relate to various, intense levels of heartbreak. Let's take a moment to reflect on the story of Job.

In the land of Uz, there lived a man whose name was Job.
This man was blameless and upright; he feared God and
shunned evil. He had seven sons and three daughters, and
he owned seven thousand sheep, three thousand camels,
five hundred yoke of oxen and five hundred donkeys, and
had a large number of servants. He was the greatest man
among all the people of the East.
Job 1:1-3, NIV

God favored Job and knew he was a faithful man. One day, the Lord spoke of him to Satan. Satan was convinced Job was only faithful because God had protected him and blessed him with many possessions, so Satan challenged God,

Marrying Freedom

*But now stretch out your hand and strike everything he
has, and he will surely curse you to your face." The Lord
said to Satan, "Very well, then, everything he has is in your
power, but on the man himself do not lay a finger.*
Job 1:11-12, NIV

Satan was ready to put Job to the test.

In one day, Job received multiple heartbreaking reports. His
oxen, donkeys, camels, sheep, servants, and ten children
were all gone. Stolen. Dead.

Wow. If just one of those situations had happened to you,
what would your reaction be? He experienced all of it within
the same twenty-four hours. And do you know what he did
in response to such agony and heartbreak?

*At this, Job got up and tore his robe and shaved his head.
Then he fell to the ground in worship and said: "Naked I
came from my mother's womb and naked I will depart. The
Lord gave and the Lord has taken away; may the name of
the Lord be praised." In all this, Job did not sin by charging
God with wrongdoing.*
Job 1:20-22, NIV

He praised the Lord. He tore his robe and shaved his head.
He fell to the ground and worshiped. Throughout all of this,
Job did not sin or blame God for anything.

Is that how you respond to challenging situations?

Your boss lets you go after ten years of slaving away to please
him . . . do you worship?
The pet you've had since you were a kid dies . . . worship?
You get a diagnosis that calls for a challenging few months of
chemo . . . worship?
The house you've spent so much time making feel like home
is robbed of everything valuable . . . worship?

When I go through heartbreak, I know worship isn't the first thing on my mind. Is it for you?

One fall afternoon, I returned from a weekend of visiting the guy I was dating and was waiting to have coffee with my mom at our local coffee shop. On the drive home, my boyfriend texted me numerous times to see if I had made it home. He had never been so quizzical about my whereabouts when I was driving, so that seemed a little odd.

That morning when I had gotten up to leave, he had walked me to my car and seemed a little quiet. However, the "I love you and see you later" was said and off I went. It was five in the morning, so I'd brushed it off. Who would be super chipper and energetic at the crack of dawn? I turned my music up and enjoyed the peaceful four-and-a-half-hour drive.

When I made it home, I texted him, and he responded with a call.

The root of the strange vibe I was feeling was clarified. His words were straight to the point. Bam! A major plot twist. "I can't do this anymore."

I was dumbfounded! How could everything have been golden over the weekend, nothing out of the ordinary, and now it was over, with no explanation as to why? I was confused on so many levels.

I was blindsided by a breakup I hadn't anticipated, and my heart was aching.

Do you think I praised God at that moment? Did I worship and thank Him for allowing a heartbreak I didn't see coming? No, far from it. I don't remember much else about that day and the week that followed—but I know there were a lot of tears and a lot of questions, "Why God?" or "Why wasn't I good enough for him?"

Just a week later, he realized "he'd made a big mistake." He pleaded for a second chance, he wouldn't mess it up this time, and he would never do that to me again, he promised.

Turns out, he had been reconnecting with his ex-girlfriend the weekend I was with him. To make matters worse, after he broke it off with me, he spent a few nights with her.

There I was shedding tears and praying about the situation, and there he was, not even thinking about me. However, that week with his ex-girlfriend made him realize he missed me and wanted to be with me.

My thoughts were, *Okay, well . . . If he spent time with her and realized he wants me, then it'd be rainbows and butterflies from then on ... right? He'd learned his lesson. He wouldn't make that mistake again.* Sureeee . . . that's what I thought would be the case.

Sometimes having a forgiving heart gets me in trouble and creates problems that are unnecessary and avoidable. I was pretty upset about it all and hated the thought of him being with someone else. Yes, it made me insecure, but if he'd decided on me, then I would be okay; it just might take some time to rebuild trust.

Oh, it's totally fine.
I missed you.
I love you, too.

I accepted him back into my life, and we talked about moving past it. It would be new waters for me—forgiving, moving forward, and forgetting. The thing was, I didn't forget what happened. I had never had to trust someone again after they'd hurt me in such a way. As time went by, I realized I couldn't seem to shake it, no matter how hard I tried.

Getting stuck in the past is what rocked my world and taught me one thing that's been a valuable lesson. In order to move past something that's caused you pain, you have to do the work to heal. You have to treat the trauma with the attention it needs. You can't get stuck in what happened and what was, and you can't get so caught up in it that it's all you think about. Looking back and working through things that happened to you is beneficial and so important.

How can you take that step if it's your first heartbreak? Or, maybe this brings to mind an incident that occurred years ago but is something you still fester on.

Take a moment to reflect and bring to light anything this topic is triggering. Uncover any ill-conceived perceptions you labeled yourself with due to bad experiences in life. How much time per day do you consciously, or even subconsciously, spend thinking about one incident or multiple different heartbreaks? Getting stuck in the pain is when problems arise and can become detrimental to your well-being.

You don't have to be a whiz to know this, but I can tell you from experience, being stuck in the past will eat at you and tear you down, until you decide to do something about it. After the reflection you just did, did you realize you too are stuck in something that happened in the past? Maybe you realized you spend way too much time contemplating it?

That's what was happening to me in this breakup. I was back in a relationship that was causing me to become more insecure by the day. I couldn't tug my thoughts away from the feeling that something still didn't seem right. I couldn't shrug it off, but I couldn't place what it was either.

On one drive to visit him, not even a month after we'd gotten back together, I remember praying to God for clarity about the relationship. "God, if he is someone I'm supposed to be with, can you somehow show me whether or not he is the right one? Give me peace about it. Help me to see and know whether I'm making the right decision."

That weekend, I got my answer.

I was getting ready to shower, and he had left his phone in

the bathroom with the music playing. As I scrolled to find a playlist to listen to, I had this overwhelming feeling I just had to look and guess what I saw . . . There, in his messages, was his ex-girlfriend's name.

I'm never one to snoop on someone, but I did something atypical that weekend.

The Lord was saying, "You wanted me to provide you with clarity. You asked, and now I'll show you."

And as much as I hate to admit what I did, I clicked on it.

Him: *I miss you.*

I scrolled a little farther.

Him: *I've been having dreams about you.*

His ex-girlfriend replied that it was wrong, but he persisted.

The following morning came with minimal sleep on my end. I couldn't ignore what was in plain sight.

When he awoke and came out to join me on the couch, I gave him a few chances to come clean, but of course, he denied any contact with her. "It's been months since I last talked to her. I deleted her number from my phone. I don't want anything to do with her."

I explained I knew he was lying because I had seen the messages.

As I finished my sentence, he began to cry. He knew this had been the last straw. Yet, he repeated it, all over again, "I didn't mean any of it. I only want you. It won't happen again. I'll delete her number. I'll block her."

La de da de da . . .

Healing After a Heartbreak

Same story, different day. Same story, same forgiving Hil.

That's right; after hashing it out, we were back to being "okay." This was his last chance, and he knew it.

Didn't I say that last time?

Things were fine for a little while: smiles, laughs, new memories, road trips, and holidays together. Yes, I felt insecure at times, thinking back to how he left me once for her and wondering if he'd blow his "last chance," but overall, things were great.

Fast forward a few months.

I was packing my things to move and start a new job. I was going to live with my sister, pursuing a job at a country club. I would be working at the golf course, which was a career goal at the time. Another perk? I was going to be living about a mile away from him. We wouldn't have to be in a long-distance relationship any longer.

As I packed my things, what do you think happened days before the move?

If you've heard the saying "history repeats itself," then you can predict what happened. He broke it off again. This time, through a text message.

This instance wasn't heartbreak. It was anger—at myself and at him. The funny thing is, what I was feeling at that point wasn't even equivalent to the anger I felt just a week later when he texted me that he wanted to meet in person and talk.

You might be thinking by now, "She better not have . . . Will she ever learn?!" Believe me; I think the same now.

Of course, silly me was forgiving enough to allow it again and still naive enough to agree to let him cook me dinner a few nights later. Would I be a girl who would allow someone who'd hurt me so much, within a five-month period of time, to have a third opportunity to hurt me?

Absolutely.

I felt like I was in a scene from a Harry Potter movie. During dinner, the name of she-who-shall-not-be-mentioned showed up, yet again, on his phone. Were we really going to bring her up at this point?

Okay, okay . . . I needed to know the truth.

"Oh, I haven't talked to her in five months, not since everything happened. I have no idea why she just randomly sent me a picture of a coffee mug that reminded her of me. She's like that and just does that kind of stuff sometimes. That's just how she is."

The next day, I responded to a message she had sent me on Instagram after the first breakup. I never responded because he convinced me to ignore it, claiming she wanted to start drama. I dug through my messages and finally sought clarification about why her name continued to pop up in his text messages each time we were together. I knew someone was lying about what was going on, and I had a feeling it was indeed him.

She asked to call me and she filled me in on the previous months of lies I'd been oblivious to. There was much more to the story than a few text messages. Much more. Including how he dropped her off from their date, right before coming to talk to me just days before.

Every single time I was with him after that moment, because yes, I was forgiving enough to maintain a friendship with him, I began questioning myself. I questioned him and everything he said to me. I hated the ache in my stomach I felt when I was with him. I knew the Lord was showing me, time and time again, he wasn't the one for me, but I kept trying to be the forgiving girl who loved him regardless of what he put me through—to show the same grace and forgiveness Jesus shows us. Every time, the thoughts would linger on ...

Why wasn't I good enough?
What was it about me that made me less appealing than this other girl?
Was I not smart enough, not pretty enough?
What was I lacking?

It's a very dangerous path to go down because, as humans, we all struggle with insecurities. We all have things that have caused us to lose a little bit of confidence in ourselves. In a committed relationship, if one party decides having just you isn't enough, well, that just magnifies and escalates those insecurities.

If you are or have ever walked through something similar, you deserve more. If you haven't, I hope you don't ever have to, but if you ever do, let me remind you—you deserve more.

You deserve a love that loves you for you, as you are, not one in which you feel you have to prove your worth. Not one in which you wonder if he's thinking about her while he's with you. Not one where your stomach is in knots every time his or her phone goes off, wondering if it's that other person again, and when he or she is going to, out of the blue, decide you're no longer good enough, and walk out the door.

I allowed myself to walk that path for much longer than I like to admit, and though I know it made me into the woman I am today, I'm not proud of it. I'm not proud of the insecurities I allowed myself to feel day after day when I knew I didn't have to. I'm not proud of the person I became during that season—shrinking myself to the lie that I wasn't worthy of something better—someone true, honest, and faithful— believing I deserved this type of relationship. What a pile of bologna that was!

Maybe it was fear . . . fear of being alone, fear of people

finding out we weren't together, fear of knowing he was with someone other than me, fear of what others would think if they knew what had happened, fear of the judgment in people's eyes when they knew I'd stuck around through all of it and still stuck up for him.

There were a lot of "things" I used to justify everything that had happened, reasons I didn't want to let go of it all, and stuck with him through it. The Lord showed me multiple times he wasn't the one for me. By sticking with him, I wasn't being obedient or trusting Him. The Lord was relentless in pursuing me and my best, and after much procrastination and stubbornness, I let Him have me. I trusted Him with it, ended the "relationship," and never looked back.

Most of us will go through heartbreak at some point in our lives, but don't let it define you for the rest of your life. Walk through those feelings, and let the Lord be the glue that puts you back together, that helps you see your true worth and value. You are not a second choice.

If you have been hurt, and you're not sure how to move on from that, seek the Lord. Those nudges He is giving you to leave or take a step back from a relationship, friendship, or career, are for a reason. We seek companionship and love from people around us, even if it's painful, because we were created to be in community and fellowship. The company we keep, though, will determine our future. The Bible warns: "Walk with the wise and become wise, for a companion of fools suffers harm" (Proverbs 13:20, NIV).

He is the Mender; allow Him to heal those pieces in your heart that are hurting. Walk through those feelings you might be experiencing, betrayal, shame, guilt, or whatever they are. Don't push them out and ignore them. Ignoring them might be easier, but by doing that, you might take unnecessary pain into the next season of life. It's time to unpack the baggage because unhealed pain could prevent you from loving and living the life you were created for. Empty the suitcase, forgive the people that hurt you, and put the bag away. Don't leave it sitting out for weeks or months with all of your dirty laundry.

You might need to pause and give yourself some time and space for Jesus to be all He wants to be for you. What if, instead of moving on right away, seeking companionship from another friend group, getting a new pet, or accepting the first job offer that comes your way, you rush into the presence of God, allowing Him to fill you up? What if, like Job, you worship the Lord through whatever is taken? It's easier said than done, but the next time you're experiencing heartbreak, why don't you give it a try? Can you look around and find at least one thing to be joyful about, that you will give a shout of praise for?

Sure, your heart may have been broken, but I know someone who can put it back together, and guess what? He loves you way more than any person or job ever could. Jesus died for you on the cross to give you life, and He loves you more in **one second** than any human being could love you in a **lifetime**. Let that sink in for a moment.

He didn't die so you would convince yourself you don't deserve love as Jesus loves us. Let His love be all you need to fill the void within you. His love is greater than any other, and He will be there beside you at your worst and once again at your best, never leaving or forsaking you for a moment in between.

Uncap the Pen:

How is your heart feeling right now? What's lying heavily on it? Is there unaddressed pain of the past that still lingers? Take a few minutes to think about the condition of your heart and soul. List five adjectives below you'd use to describe your current state.

____

____

____

Do you know the root of these emotions? Is it a person, a place, or an activity that is causing your heart and soul to feel this way? What do you need right now? Is it mending, is it comfort, is it peace of mind? Write out a prayer below for Jesus to be those things you are needing.

____

____

____

____

____

Jot out any thoughts you have after reading this chapter. Have you had your heart broken? Have you broken another's heart? List out the feelings you experienced during that time.

____

____

____

____

____

Healing After a Heartbreak

Write what you'd like to say to Jesus, to the one who hurt you, to the one you hurt. Don't bottle it up any longer. Let it out, and let Him be the one who fills you back up after it's all out. Try not to ponder or come back to these thoughts once you finally release them to the Lord.

____

____

____

____

____

____

____

<u>Sign the Divorce Papers:</u>

"Lord, I know You are all that I need. I know my value and worth come from You and You alone. You provide fulfillment and peace. You mend every broken heart; You are the healing through our darkest seasons, our joy and light. You are everything we need, and I pray You would be that to me right now. I don't want the hurt and heartbreak to hinder me any longer. I might not know what my heart needs or even what I need to pray for, but You know, Lord. You know what I want and what I need, and I pray that right now, you would Help me find contentment and wholeness in You alone. Thank You for loving me fiercely and unconditionally. Help me to see myself as You see me and to recognize my value and worth, so I can live a life reflective of that. I love You, Lord."

Marrying Freedom

Remaining Expectant After Disappointment

*"For my thoughts are not your thoughts, neither are your
ways my ways," declares the Lord. "As the heavens are
higher than the earth, so are my ways higher than your
ways and my thoughts than your thoughts."*
Isaiah 55:8-9, NIV

When we get our hopes up, there's always a chance we can
be disappointed. Maybe it's because whatever we'd hoped for
didn't take place, or the plans we made changed; nevertheless,
this can plant roots of disappointment within us.

As I was growing up and faced what seemed like one
disappointment after another, I stopped getting my hopes
up. I became convinced that if I cared too much, I might
jinx things.

When I was on the East Coast for work a couple of summers
back, my parents and brother were supposed to come visit
me while my team and I were in Washington, D.C. My family
had never been to D.C. before, so I was over the moon about
them coming to see the city. It had been a few months since
I'd last seen them, and I was going to be in town for about
a week, with a few days off work. It was going to be perfect.

The day before they were supposed to come, my brother
was to visit my grandma and get her laundry so they could
take care of things for her before they left. She wasn't
answering her phone, so my mom thought maybe she had
gone down to do a load herself. She always sat with the
laundry when she washed. A couple of hours passed . . . still
no answer. Mom was out on her mail route with the only set
of keys to check up on Grandma. Therefore, my mom told
my brother to call the police to request a wellness check
because that was the only way he'd be able to get in.

As soon as they entered her home, they found Grandma on

the bathroom floor. She had had a stroke. She was airlifted to the nearest hospital and made it through, but was paralyzed and bound to a wheelchair for the rest of her days.

Needless to say, they didn't make the trip to D.C., and I was twelve hours away, terrified about what was going on. There was nothing I could do and no quick magic button to press to take me back home.

A few months after, when I returned home, I was feeling overwhelmed. There was discord in some personal relationships, and I was feeling the weight of it all. I'd decided I needed some time away to recharge, so I booked a last-minute trip to see my friend in California. The flight was super affordable and scheduled to depart the following morning. We were beyond excited because it had been two years since I'd last seen her. I packed my bags and went off to sleep, anticipating the following morning. A few hours later, I woke up and could not stop throwing up. The sickness lasted all night, and by the time the hour arrived to leave for the airport, I couldn't stomach the thought of being on a plane for four hours, not to mention the two-hour drive to the airport. Thank goodness for full refunds on cancellations made within twenty-four hours of booking.

The disappointment continued.

When COVID arrived in early 2020, the opportunity to visit family in nursing homes was restricted for over a year. My grandma was confined to her room. Her space was on the side of the building that overlooked a patio, but visitors didn't have access to it without going through the building, so there wasn't even the opportunity to wave to her through a window. The day FINALLY arrived, almost a year later, when they lessened restrictions, and we could go visit her. We scheduled our appointment and ventured to see her one Saturday afternoon. As soon as they wheeled Grandma up, my husband and I knew something was wrong. She barely opened her eyes while we were sitting there, and her breathing sounded labored and shallow. Within four days, she was gone. I didn't even get to tell her about our wedding and show her pictures as I had planned.

You get the picture.

Hope. Anticipation. Excitement. Disappointment.

Are you familiar with the phrase, "Expectation is the root of all heartache?"

That phrase became planted in my heart. Don't get your hopes up, don't expect anything, don't get excited . . . that way, you won't be disappointed if it doesn't work out.

Before my husband and I began dating, we had lunch every Saturday. After work, we would go grab lunch or coffee then go our separate ways. One Saturday, we decided to go to Target after lunch. I know, I know; a guy's dream outing. As we were walking around, chatting, we somehow got on the topic of expectation and disappointment. I told him I didn't get my hopes up for anything because that way, whether it works out or it doesn't, I won't be disappointed.

I was convinced that by getting my hopes up, I'd for sure jinx whatever I was hopeful for. I remember him telling me that living that way was no way to live. Yes, I knew that, but that didn't mean it was an easy fix. It had been a way of living I had grown accustomed to for years. I couldn't just release that pattern of thinking right after that conversation; I knew it would take some work.

The more I dug into my thought patterns, I realized I was half-living, almost walking through the motions. Instead of embracing every season and what it brought, I was detached from any of my hopes. Life had shown me, time and time again, living in expectation was a gamble. Therefore, I just stopped hoping altogether. I didn't want to jinx even the possibility of something playing out, so, I began living life and my day-to-day "on-the-fly."

Planning a trip? Schedule it at the last second. That way, there's very little time for it not to work out.

Going on a date? Plan it moments before, and don't talk about the details in advance. That way, I won't be disappointed when something comes up or he "forgot" he had plans.

Applying for a new opportunity? Oh, it seems great but just wait to see what happens. Even if it seems to be the perfect fit and everything is awesome, just imagining myself in that role and getting excited about it could jinx my chances.

How ridiculous does that sound?

Well, it was my life painted in a picture, and it was not a pretty picture. It wasn't a mural I wanted to hang on the wall of a cozy living room. However, knowing that I shouldn't live in that thought pattern and trying not to live like that were two very different, challenging tasks. I knew that through Jesus, we can all have hope. We see encouragement in Scripture:

For in this hope we were saved. But hope that is seen is no hope at all. Who hopes for what they already have? But if we hope for what we do not yet have, we wait for it patiently.
Romans 8:24-25, NIV

We must wait for what we do not yet have. Patiently.

But how do we even wait patiently and expectantly? What does that look like in the life of a young adult? In the life of an older man or woman? What about waiting for something for months or years, with all signs indicating it's never going to happen?

The hard truth I've learned is, well, it just might not happen.

You might not get that job.
You might not marry that person.
You might not get to go away for the weekend.
You might not get into the college you were banking on

attending.

You just might not get what you were hoping for.

There was a time when I went to visit a friend for the weekend. I'd known him our entire lives, and our friendship had grown over the previous months, exchanging phone calls and texts and spending time together. I was excited and expectant about what was to come in the future, even pondering the fact that maybe, just maybe, he could be my future husband. Each and every day, I continued to hand it over to the Lord. Whether we would be more than what we were or not, He would arrange it. He could bring it if it were to be.

A previous heartbreak played a huge role in how independent and detached I'd become, but after many heart-to-hearts and sweet conversations, this friendship taught me something important. I came face to face with the fact I'd been fearful, closed off, and afraid of opening my heart to anyone or anything. I was careful about who I opened up to and didn't trust quickly at all. I often questioned people's intentions. I was as detached as detached could be.

As our friendship grew, I was reminded there are amazing people out there, that it's good to have expectations and hope and to experience the smiles, love, and laughter that others can bring to our lives. I was avoiding that, and by doing so, I was missing so much. There is so much more to life—so much love to give, smiles to cause, hugs to share, and lessons to learn that will mold us and shape us into the people God created us to be. Taking a chance results in an abundance of living that we would otherwise miss.

The weekend arrived, and as I drove three hours to visit him, I felt my heart growing more excited as I got closer. I couldn't wait to see what the weekend would bring. It'd be a weekend together in the beautiful city of Madison, Wisconsin, a city I'd never visited. I'd be with someone who was helping me see new perspectives on life. After a few busy months of being apart, it was going to be the best weekend ever.

Marrying Freedom

That's how it started, anyway.

On the blustery winter day, we ventured out to explore. He showed me around the University's campus and the beauty of Wisconsin. We caught up on life, job searches, his mission trip, and all that had been going on. I'd been working crazy hours, so I gladly welcomed binging a reality TV show and staying cozy for a few hours of the day. Maybe it was the flow of the conversation or the way his demeanor changed, but about midway through the weekend, I got the sense that "friends" was all we'd ever be. I'd been journaling and praying about marrying this man, so coming to that realization wasn't a reality I was quite ready to face. I shrugged it off and tried to enjoy the remaining time.

However, before I headed home on Sunday, he said he wanted to talk to me about something.

I knew the words I didn't want to hear were coming, and they did. The hard truth was, the timing wasn't right for us to be anything more than friends.

It was great to have clarity, yet knowing that truth didn't make it any easier. I went to a Starbucks before I made my way home. It was a rainy, dreary day on a Sunday, after church, so there were floods of families and couples getting coffee together.

I nestled up in a corner with a book, my journal, and a cup of coffee, and turned my music up on my headphones to block out the rest of the world. I couldn't look around because the sight of happy families saddened me to the core, and I knew it would cause the tears to stream if I took a good look at all of their smiling faces. What I desired more than anything was all around me, and there I was, the absolute farthest I could be from having any of that for myself.

Tears welled up in my eyes as I spilled out my heart to Jesus in my journal:

Remaining Expectant After Disappointment

"Ahhh. God. I know you are all that I need, but the sting of rejection pierces deep. As I sit in Starbucks, I see couples, families, babies ... The things I yearn for so badly, and yet, I am so far from at this moment. Give me peace and joy in You. Can you be my true source of joy? I know you have the best in store. Help me to trust and believe it and wait in joyful expectation with no doubts. I need your strength, badly."

Maybe I saw it coming, maybe I knew it wasn't going to progress into a relationship, but I had allowed hope in and opened my heart again for the first time in a while. I was disappointed and saddened because I knew that meant I'd have to be vulnerable and open up to someone else in the future. Even worse, I wondered where in the world I would even find a decent man.

This was disappointing, but for once, I realized, after some thought, I wasn't crushed by it. Instead, I discerned I was sad for the what-ifs and the could-have-beens, yet, somehow, still hopeful.

The next day, I could feel a shift in my perspective and energy. The start of my journal entry looked a tad bit different than just twenty-four hours earlier:

"Every day I need you. Be my peace, fulfillment, and direction. Am I sort of at peace because I know you are working behind the scenes right now for the good? I trust you and surrender it all to you."

Wait, what? How did I end up feeling at peace after someone I cared about decided that he needed to go his separate way?

Even though I respect this great man, I knew God had something better for me. I just needed to keep being patient, hopeful, and faithful in my waiting. Rather than letting disappointment take root in my heart, the Lord showed me a newfound hope. He showed me the beauty of taking chances, of loving without fear, of embracing the opportunities, the people, and the challenges that this life brings. Sure, they might result in disappointment, but boy, the journey is still full of beauty.

Had He done work on my heart or what?! This was the complete opposite of how I'd felt in the past. I realized that through the disappointments I'd faced, I had grown. I didn't let what turned out differently than I'd hoped to make me bitter and dejected. I learned to look at those disappointments from a fresh perspective. Sure, it might sting and hurt for a little bit and mean I have to wait even longer, but the Lord was preparing me for His promises and what He had in store.

It's like the story of the lost donkeys in 1 Samuel 9. The donkeys of Saul's father, Kish, were lost. He sent Saul out to look for them. He looked in town after town to no avail. He decided it was time to head back home before his father started to worry about him. As a last resort, the servant with him suggested, "Look, in this town there is a man of God; he is highly respected, and everything he says comes true. Let's go there now. Perhaps he will tell us which way we should go" (1 Samuel 9:6, NIV). Saul agreed that it was their last shot.

Little did Saul know, the Lord had informed Samuel the day before, "About this time tomorrow I will send you a man from the land of Benjamin. Anoint him ruler over my people Israel; he will deliver them from the hand of the Philistines" (1 Samuel 9:16, NIV).

Saul thought he was wandering and looking for the lost donkeys, but God had sent him to Samuel, and there was a much greater purpose than what he thought. The disappointment was laying the groundwork for a greater appointment for Saul's life: he would one day become king of Israel.

God is always at work. Even when you feel frustrated, discouraged, and have little hope remaining. It's tough to remain strong and hopeful, even more, when you face disappointment after disappointment. Saul couldn't catch a break. He searched for those donkeys but kept hitting a wall. We have all been through similar seasons, feeling like it's hopeless and as if we just cannot catch our footing. You may feel that way right now. In those moments, remain steadfast and trust in God's perfect timing, His promises, and His faithfulness. Yes, it's easier said than done, but keep holding on. Keep trusting, and keep stepping one foot in front of the other.

If He's placed something in your heart, it's for a good reason. Whether it's a certain type of career, schooling, relationship, marriage, friendship, trip, or whatever hope you have tugging on your heart, there is a reason for that, just as there is a reason for every "no" or change in plans that comes your way. Don't be afraid to get your hopes up and believe God for it.

If the results are different than you'd hoped, anticipated, or planned for, don't let that get you down. Don't let the enemy slip into your mind and tell you it isn't worth it, that it isn't going to happen, or that you're a failure. Don't let him squeeze his way in because he WILL try. He will use every teeny, tiny lie he can to get into your head and get you down in the dumps.

You have to recognize that and know he will try with every fiber of his being to infiltrate your efforts. Disappointments do sting and can make you feel defeated. The Devil knows that very well, and so there he will be, right beside you. He'll try with all his might to overpower your thoughts of perseverance and hope. Don't let defeat, frustration, or depression take root.

Get out your umbrella for when the Devil tries to rain down on you. He'll send the darkest clouds and pour out every trick in his book to try to drown and overpower you. Let those lies fall on and away from your umbrella, sinking into a desert ground, desperate for water that will soak up every lie mumbled. Stand tall and strong on the word of God and believe the Lord for His faithfulness. Has He been faithful to you in the past? Has he come through for you in other situations? He WILL do it again.

If those disappointments hurt you; if you're mad, tell Him how you're feeling. He wants you to come to Him; He wants you to talk to Him. Make an appointment with Him to share the feelings of disappointment. He knows your heart, but He wants to hear it. For every disappointment you and I face, we can rest assured that there is something better coming, and He withholds no good thing. You must learn to be expectant and joyful in the process, finding hope and peace in the Lord, and trusting He will provide the best in His timing.

Remember, disappointment doesn't define you. It doesn't mean you aren't worthy, not good enough, or of too little value to attain what you were hoping for. Disappointment means God has a divine appointment in mind for something better. It might not make sense now, and it might feel like you're walking town to town searching for lost donkeys but hold tight. God has it in His calendar, scheduled to the exact time and date. It is going to be amazing. Keep hoping, and continue stepping into your future day by day. As God fulfilled His plans for Saul through the lost donkeys, He is orchestrating your every moment behind the scenes too. Cling to His promises. The best is yet to come!

Uncap the Pen:

In your life, do you avoid getting your hopes up to avoid disappointment, or do you get excited when a setback strikes? Explain your thoughts.

____

____

____

____

Remaining Expectant After Disappointment

Take a few minutes to think about the things that have disappointed you most recently. Is there a disappointment you just can't seem to shake? Discuss the situation.

____

____

____

Next, think back through your lifetime. Write a few things that have caused you hurt feelings or feelings of disappointment that might have caused you to lose hope in someone or something.

____

____

____

Now, see those disappointments from a new perspective. Take a few minutes to consider the good that came out of that situation or a way that you could look at it with optimism. Did you grow as a person? Was your family changed by it? Did that "no" lead you to something completely different and more fitting for you? No matter how difficult it was, try to see at least one good thing that came from your times of dismay.

____

____

____

____

<u>Sign the Divorce Papers:</u>

"Lord, disappointment stings. Truthfully, sometimes it is hard to let go and trust You to move. Sometimes it's hard to remain hopeful when it seems I face trial after trial, disappointment after disappointment. Help me believe You won't withhold any good thing from me. Help me remain strong and persistent in my journey to become the person You created me to be. With every setback, help me bounce back with new hope and excitement. Let me be led by the promise of Your goodness and faithfulness, regardless of how bleak the situations, hopes, or dreams appear to my earthly mind. You are good, Father, and I thank you for every disappointment that led me to your perfect plan. Thank You, Jesus, for knowing better than me. I love You, Lord.

Triumphing Over Temptation

*No temptation has overtaken you except what is
common to mankind. And God is faithful; he will not let
you be tempted beyond what you can bear. But when you
are tempted, he will also provide a way out
so that you can endure it.*
1 Corinthians 10:13, NIV

"Do you know how good you would feel if you did that?!"
How many times have you thought this?

Our thoughts and feelings sway us, persuade us, and
sometimes cause us to do things we may not be proud of
the following day.

*You should have one more piece of cake. It is a special
occasion, so you might as well overindulge. There isn't an
opportunity for cake every day. You've got to take advantage
of it while it's here.*

*Your wife is out of town for the week, and I know you're
going to get lonely. It's okay to go sit at the bar for a couple
of hours and flirt with the bartender. Your wife will never
know, and if you "forget" to wear your ring, the bartender
will never even know you're married, so no harm done.*

*You can read your devotion tomorrow. You'll have more
time. You need to finish this series on Netflix tonight.*

*You're planning to marry her. It's okay to sleep with her. Even
if it doesn't work out in the end, you love her right now, and
that's all that really matters.*

*Your family is here, vying for your attention, but just five
more minutes scrolling through Facebook. You don't want to
miss any important life updates from your friends. You can
spend quality, devoted time with your family later.*

It's rainy out today. You're feeling lazy. You don't need to clean the house. Sure, it's a mess, but maybe another day. It can wait.

Just a few minutes of the porn you came across online won't hurt. It's from the comfort of your room, so no one will even know.

Man, isn't the Devil sly? He knows all of the tricks, the tiny little whispers and tactics. Before we know it, we won't even think twice. We'll give in to something we know we shouldn't. He'll do it to us without us even realizing it. He knows our weaknesses, our struggles, and what pushes our buttons. He knows exactly what he needs to say that will trick us into believing that whatever we're contemplating is okay. Sooner or later, listening to those little lies will get us into a bind of some sort.

Temptation comes in many forms: sexual temptation, the temptation to worry, overindulgence in food, procrastination, social media overuse, and laziness . . . The enemy has a line for any and every situation, and more often than not, we fall for his smooth talking.

"Just this one time. No one will ever find out." That's how he lures us in . . . Just this once.

You negotiate with yourself and convince yourself that contrary to what you actually believe, just this time wouldn't hurt. What's one little time? And so, you give in.

But, once turns into twice, and twice into a handful of times, and before you know it, you can't stop.

Each time, you say this is the last time; however, each time, you find it harder and harder to stop. You keep creating justifications in your head as to why what you're doing is okay. You continue to fall deeper into a pit without the slightest realization of what it's doing to you.

Triumphing Over Temptation

How many times have you watched something on Netflix and said, "Just one more episode." Before you know it, three hours have gone by, and you're mid-season on the newest release. I'm guilty of it. Last weekend, I did that with a book. I kept telling myself, "One more chapter." Then, before I knew it, it was 11:30 p.m., and I needed to get up early the next morning. It's easy to do. It's easy to say just one more ______ and keep on saying it without any true end in sight.

I've wasted hours just mindlessly watching episode after episode of *Gossip Girl*. I've allowed social media to take up too much of my time and been lured into the "I love you, so why can't we" trap. There are times I've kept eating when I knew I should stop; I've created excuses in my head as to why I don't need to exercise today . . . I could go on and on about the ways I've fallen into a variety of temptations more than once. You aren't alone in this, friend.

Oftentimes, there is a part of us that feels slightly guilty about a decision; especially if we realize we're creating justifications for something in our minds. We don't share that side of ourselves with anyone because we believe it will be fine. We rationalize it, and it makes sense to us. If we keep it to ourselves, and if we don't talk about the details of it with anyone, it takes away some of the impact that it's actually having on us. Keeping it quiet helps us cope because if we actually spoke about it out loud, it might seem more real. If it were real, then that would mean we would have to think about the consequences and what it's doing to our hearts, mind, and soul.

When we find ourselves walking through a season of temptation, it's easy to want to be alone with our thoughts, to avoid the people we know will call us out or will see through the facade we try to put on. It's easier to be alone because then it doesn't have to be talked about. Sure, having no accountability makes things less challenging, but that's also the most dangerous place. It's tricky to triumph over temptation if you try to tackle it alone.

Sometimes you might need your space to work through things, but you must be extremely careful in those moments because that's often the time the enemy will use his tactics to creep in and tell you, "Just this one time won't be bad. Go ahead and do it. You'll enjoy it." You have no one to hold you accountable, so the enemy wins. You experience the fleeting pleasure that comes with your vices and begin to justify your behavior, "If I do this, God's grace is never-ending, and He will forgive me."

So, you do it once. Then, the next time, you find it a little easier to carry it out. Your decision process becomes clearer; you'll keep going for it. The pleasure comes, but sometimes you don't realize the chains wrapping around you tighter and tighter. You might feel guilty every now and then and consider trying to break free from it but never put any effort into it. You've fallen deeper and deeper down the rabbit hole now. You convince yourself it's all good because God will keep forgiving you.

Yikes.

I'm sure we can all agree we've done something we knew was wrong when doing it. However, we were alone or were with people who encouraged the act, so we felt as if that made it a little better.

What isn't seen, isn't really wrong, right?
If no one finds out, then it's not sinning.
If they're doing it, then I can do it; it's fine.

The thing is, sinning is sin, whether done where no one can see or in a room full of people. Partial disobedience is still disobedience, and there is no sin that is greater or worse than another sin.

That phrase is one that always gets me. If all sins are equal, lying is the same as killing. Coveting your neighbor's goods is equal to committing adultery. Sinning is sinning, and just because everyone else is doing it, doesn't make it any more right.

Triumphing Over Temptation

Let's say you and all of your friends are out at the mall, and each of them sneaks some makeup items into their pockets and walks out, and everyone gets away with it. No harm was done; no one was caught. But the lack of alarms and no one getting caught doesn't make it okay.

You're out to dinner, and everyone else decides to have too much to drink. You don't want to be the oddball out, so you, too, overindulge in beverages. Before you know it, you can barely walk straight, let alone wake up early the next morning to meet your family for the holiday meal.

We all have temptations and vices in our lives, things that we turn to, fall into, and keep going back to. It might be a small thing in your mind, or it might seem like a huge deal that you can't escape—one that you want to break free from, but you find it so difficult. The temptations might ebb and flow with the seasons of your life.

When you're in junior high, it might be tempting to cheat on an exam.

In high school, the temptation to give your body to your date at the high school prom.

In college, drinking and drugs.

In the workplace, scheming and not telling the full truth in order to earn a few extra bucks.

In a marriage, having friendships that get just a little too friendly sometimes when no one else is around or having a secret addiction to pornography.

Temptation could be a life-long struggle, beginning and ending at any given age. Some might struggle with multiple temptations; some could just have one temptation that they can't escape.

At any age, there are likely to be things we face where doing what's "right" is contrary to culture.

As a young adult in our generation, it's easy to see the media is over-sexualized. Many TV shows flaunt characters sleeping around with one another. The virgin is made fun of. Sex is cool, fun, and casual, with no consequences—at least, that's what our society has come to teach.

What does the Word of God say?

"Therefore a man shall leave his father and his mother and hold fast to his wife, and they shall become one flesh."
Genesis 2:24-25, NIV

It doesn't say, a man meets a girl, dates her for a week, and they become one. Or, a man becomes one with a girl he just met. But we see college parties turn into late nights and hookups, and more often than not, many people around us are giving themselves away as we see on TV: casually, sometimes even meaninglessly.

I grew up going to a Catholic school from Pre-K through 8th grade, so you might say I was a tad bit sheltered. Once high school hit, it was like a whole new world of information. I played on the varsity volleyball team my sophomore year, and that was a very eye-opening year, to say the least.

I remember one day at practice, the girls were talking about the guys they were dating and doing all of these things I had never even heard of. I had no idea what they were saying half the time. All I did know for certain was I felt extremely uncomfortable whenever they asked why I wasn't having sex with my boyfriend, even though we'd been dating for over a year.

Growing up, it was my plan to wait until I was married. That's what I'd been taught, that's what I believed in, and I knew deep in my heart, that was truly what I wanted. We even signed these little pledge cards at a presentation we had to listen to in eighth grade, vowing that we'd save ourselves for marriage, and I was all in.

Triumphing Over Temptation

It's easy to want something for yourself, but it becomes much harder when you are surrounded by people who believe or are practicing something completely opposite of you. It can be lonely, terrifying, and intimidating. You can feel as if others are looking down on you or talking about you because you're doing something different than them. That comes with anything: with your job, your friends, your lifestyle, you name it. If you're living differently, it's going to come at a cost, and people are probably going to talk.

There are lots of emotions that it can evoke, and no, it's not easy, and it's not fun. It can lead you to do things you're not proud of down the road, or it can cause others to do or say things to you because they want you to feel a certain way about yourself for not being like them. It truly is so hard, but believe me when I say, it is not your fault, and it has nothing to do with you. If someone is coming at you with how you are living, it's most likely because they are insecure, they're unhappy, or some other internal motivator. It isn't you.

One Saturday morning, I remember waking up and looking outside. From the porch, it looked like there was something all over my car windows. I went out to see what it was, and all of the back windows were covered in derogatory hurtful words: Slut. Whore. And worse. They were awful words girls from school wanted to say about me, regardless of how far from the truth it was. Words that stung, that made me feel even more out of place. I was mortified.

It wasn't long before I let the pressure get to me . . . the pressure from comments of those around me, the pressures and arguments that arose from my then boyfriend of a year-and-a-half. It wasn't anyone's business, but that was high school for me in a small town. Everyone knew everything, whether you wanted them to or not. I started looking at sex as "I just need to get it over with, to give in to him so that everyone will lay off."

Can I tell you how awful I felt, especially when I looked at it that way? God created sex to be something special and honoring between a husband and a wife, and I was seeing it, instead, as something to "just get over with." It was a distorted view that I'd come to believe was common and right, but it sure didn't feel right. Yes, I "loved" him, but I sure didn't love what decisions I would make because of that.

I knew the Lord didn't want that for me. I didn't even want it for myself. Yet, I let society convince me that in order for someone to love me, in order for someone to want to be with me, in order to be like everyone else and fit in, I had to do it. What a far cry from the truth. I was aware of it and knew deep in my heart it was wrong, but I allowed the lies and pressures to get to me.

If I could go back and tell younger me what I know now, the decisions I made back then would look a lot different. I know she would have stood up for her beliefs. She'd have stayed strong and not given in to the peer pressure around her. I know she wouldn't have cared about what she had to face because she was different. She would have kept doing her thing. She'd have let the guys go, easily, who stopped talking to her because she wouldn't sleep with them. She'd have persisted through it all. She would have remembered Jesus' temptation in the wilderness. She would have told the Devil to back off and get away, just like Jesus did:

Then Jesus was led by the Spirit into the wilderness to be tempted by the devil. After fasting forty days and forty nights, he was hungry. The tempter came to him and said, "If you are the Son of God, tell these stones to become bread."

Jesus answered, "It is written: 'Man shall not live on bread alone, but on every word that comes from the mouth of God."

Then the devil took him to the holy city and had him stand on the highest point of the temple. "If you are the Son of God," he said, "throw yourself down. For it is written: "'He will command his angels concerning you, and they will lift you up in their hands, so that you will not strike your foot against a stone." Jesus answered him, "It is also written: 'Do not put the Lord your God to the test."

Again, the devil took him to a very high mountain and showed him all the kingdoms of the world and their splendor. "All this I will give you," he said, "if you will bow down and worship me."

Jesus said to him, "Away from me, Satan! For it is written: 'Worship the Lord your God, and serve him only."
Then the devil left him, and angels came and attended him.
Matthew 4:1-11, NIV

Three times in a row, the Devil persists. Three times, Jesus overcomes the temptation. He didn't give in. We have that same power living inside of us. If you're in the boat that Jesus was in, stay strong. If you're debating whether to stick to what you believe and want for yourself or whether you should give in and follow the crowd, stand your ground. And no, this doesn't have to be solely about sexual sins; it can be anything.

These temptations we face and struggle with might be strong, but they don't hold a power stronger than the Lord's hand on us. He is holding us in His hands, and He lives in us. In His power and strength, He performed miracles. He was faced with temptation yet never sinned; He rose from the dead. That same power of the Lord lives right inside our hearts. It's through our strength, paired with the Lord's, that we can take control and overcome these temptations. It's with Him that we can be stronger than the things that, in our minds, seem impossible to overcome.

Stand up for what you believe in. Stay firm in it, no matter what it is or how hard it gets. Find people that will support you and have similar beliefs. There will always be people who try to sway you away, so be cautious of who you surround yourself with. Find your circle, and lean into them, seek accountability, study up on God's word, and don't compromise. Stand firm. It will be worth it in the end.

But friend, you must be prepared—you might have to go

through some really hard and ugly times. There will be people who will walk out of your life because they do not hold the same values or priorities as you. Let them walk. People may make fun of you, slander you, post mean things about you, and hurt your heart and soul. Remember who God says you are. Stay true to yourself. The Lord will fill that void; He will bring you peace, joy, courage, and comfort, and He'll fill your life with the ones that you need.

There will be people who try to convince you to stay chained to your temptation. They will say, "Well, you already did it. You're stuck in your cycle. There's no hope for you." I'm here to tell you: THOSE WHO SAY THAT ARE WRONG!! You see, what was beautiful in my situation was God's grace and the work He did in my heart after my decision was made to give into the temptation. For each decision I made that was the opposite of what I knew God created for me and for my future marriage, I felt His mercy, His grace, and His nudging me back to Him. Though it may have been done, and I may have fallen off the path He had for me for quite some time, that didn't mean I had to remain in that pattern of temptation and sin and that I had to see sex as everyone around me saw it. To me, it was something more; it was a treasure and something special.

The day I finally made the decision that I would refrain from that temptation again until I was married, it felt like a weight lifted off of my shoulder. No, it hasn't always been easy. No, I wasn't always perfect. No, not every person will agree or has agreed with my decision. Yes, there have been guys who have completely stopped talking to me once they knew I wouldn't sleep with them. Do you know how I felt about that? If that's the one thing that prevented someone from continuing a relationship with me, I was totally fine with letting them go. I even started to find humor in it.

I knew that if someone was trying to persuade me of all of the reasons why I shouldn't wait until I was married, then that was not the person for me. When I was writing this book, I knew wholeheartedly that the man I would marry would respect my decision. I believed he would honor it, encourage it, and would want that for me and for us.

As I work through my edits almost two years later, guess what? The man I married did exactly that. He knew before I even told him that I wanted to wait. He respected it. He encouraged it. He wanted the same for us. Not once did he ever try to pressure me to change my mind. No, it wasn't always easy, but it was well worth it, and our marriage is stronger because of it.

The thing is, there are temptations we all have, and we are usually aware of what causes us to struggle. I knew mine was influenced by the people I was around, the stuff I listened to, the shows I consumed, and the things I did in my free time. Are you aware of what causes you or influences you to trip up, to sway your actions one way or the other? You must take actions that will prevent you from being in those circumstances.

If it's something you've struggled with for a while, it isn't going to automatically be a vice that doesn't faze you anymore. Do not be defeated by that. Don't be discouraged if you still struggle, if you find yourself falling back into it. You didn't develop that habit, that pattern, overnight, and it probably won't disappear overnight. It might take some time. It will take clinging to Jesus to find the strength not to give in to whatever temptation you're facing. Remember, "No temptation has overtaken you except what is common to mankind. And God is faithful; he will not let you be tempted beyond what you can bear. But when you are tempted, he will also provide a way out so that you can endure it. He will provide you a way out" (1 Corinthians 10:13, NIV).

It's easy to want to go back to whatever your vice is. It's comfortable. It may be something that's had a hold on you for years, so it just feels right to have it in your life. It might be something that feels good at the time, but the pleasure is fleeting and emptying to your soul. You feel afraid and challenged, and don't know what life will be like once you break free, so you still let it creep in every now and then.

Whether we're talking about foods, behavior patterns, laziness, drunkenness, thoughts, words, actions, or whichever category your struggle or struggles fall into, the first step is to recognize and admit it. Then, you have to decide. Decide you want to divorce that vice. Sign it over, and give all custody to God. Know that the journey won't be easy, but also, have faith that our God is bigger. He's greater. He's stronger. He's all-knowing. He's Redeemer. He's a Fighter. He'll help you fight your battles. He'll help you triumph over the most tempting situations. He's not going to let you remain tied to this. Take it one step, one day at a time, and show yourself grace.

Next time you're deciding whether you want to fall back into your old ways because it's comfortable or to run to Jesus, remember, He is the Guide. He knows the blueprints, the path that led you to this, and He has the roadmap for getting you out of it. He'll navigate you through the desert and away from every temptation you face. You'll be able to look back as you drive away waving, "So long, old foe. I won't be seeing you again."

Uncap the Pen:

Are there certain temptations in your life that you struggle with? List them below, no matter how ashamed or guilty you may feel, no matter how much or how little you'd like to admit that this is something you struggle with.

____

____

____

Triumphing Over Temptation

Think about how long this has been something that's been controlling you and your life. Maybe you never considered it a temptation but have realized, over time, that it is unhealthy for you. What sparked it, and how long have you been battling it?

____

____

____

What is a healthy alternative to turn to when you are faced with this temptation? Is there an action you can take, a friend you can turn to that will hold you accountable? List it below.

____

____

____

Write down a verse you can cling to when the temptation comes your way. The Lord gives us strength. Let His word be the guide that helps you sail away from those strongholds in your life.

____

____

____

<u>Sign the Divorce Papers:</u>

"Lord, You know my struggles. You know that when the temptation comes, it's SO easy for me to fall back into it. It's easy because it's comfortable, and it's been a part of my life for so long. I don't want to turn to these vices any longer. I don't want to be controlled by them. Give me strength to overcome _______________ (insert your temptations). I'm signing it over to you. The custody is Yours. Give me the strength not to give up. Direct my thoughts, words, and actions so they honor You and bring You glory. May my journey be a testimony to those around me that it is indeed possible to overcome anything through You and with You. Thank You for never leaving me, and thank You for making me strong in You."

Filling Your Soul Instead of Striving for Status

He says, "Be still, and know that I am God;
I will be exalted among the nations,
I will be exalted in the earth."
Psalm 46:10, NIV

What gets you out of bed in the morning?

Is it a paycheck? Is it pure enjoyment for what you do? Is it time with your family and friends?

For a majority, the morning means it's time to get up and head off to work, whether that work is indeed enjoyable or dreadful.

For as long as I can remember, I've been a striving perfectionist. I received straight A's not only in high school but in college as well. I spent the majority of my time studying. When I wasn't studying, I was worrying about the next moment I could sit down to open my books again. Looking back, it's kind of pathetic. Did I get good grades? Absolutely. Could I have balanced my time a little better? You bet.

Reaching for earthly success was something that was very important to me, at the time.

Can you relate to any of the following:
- Working long hours to earn a few extra dollars, all at the expense of time with the loved ones in your life?
- Studying late into the night and cramming every last second into preparation for a midterm, causing you to become sick from exhaustion?
- Striving towards that next level of success, thinking once you get there, you will be able to take a break and enjoy where you are. However, once you reach that next step, you often find yourself gazing toward grandeur, dreaming about what comes next?

When did we stop living with contentment and gratitude? We've gone from being grateful to craving more. We focus our eyes on that next rung on the ladder—the next goal, promotion, or opportunity.

Since graduating from college, I've journeyed here, there, and everywhere. I've worked long days, weeks, and months at a time, justifying that "this contract won't last forever, so I might as well enjoy it now." In a recent job, I was leaving before dawn, getting home late, and trying to squeeze in sporadic minutes to pursue the passions in my heart. It was problematic because I was exhausted and unfocused by the time I finished everything the day entailed.

One day, I got home around 4 p.m. On a normal day, I would take a little break, eat a snack, chat with my parents, and get right on my computer for a couple of hours. It's ingrained in my mind that if I'm awake, I need to be working or doing something; therefore, it's unheard of for me to go home and not do "work" of some sort.

That particular afternoon, I knew I couldn't do it. My brain was fried, and I was certain I couldn't open my computer and produce quality content. I'd been on the go for the previous two weeks. It was time to prioritize my mental health. My racing thoughts needed to be subdued, so I did the thing I crave when I get overwhelmed—I sat outside in the sunshine and soaked up the rays on the beautiful, toasty summer day. I closed my eyes and let the sound of the birds chirping and the farm animals coming in for food fill my mind. Whenever my mind is racing, nature is the one thing that can slow it down.

I took my Bible out to the deck and opened it up. I flipped it open, and it happened to land on Colossians. My favorite verse is nestled in the middle of that book, "Whatever you do, work at it with all your heart, as working for the Lord, not for human masters" (Colossians 3:23, NIV). It's a great reminder to me that whatever I'm doing, whether I enjoy it or not, to do it with an attitude of doing it for the Lord. When I read the chapter from the beginning on that certain day, I was seeing it with fresh eyes.

I'd been on the go, saying yes to anything and everything, keeping busy. But, had I been saying yes and agreeing to those things because I wanted to, or because I felt an unspoken expectation to do so? Was I keeping busy out of the notion that busy meant money and money meant success, which meant approval and promotion? Or, was I keeping busy doing things that would further my talent, wisdom, and knowledge, molding me into a sharper tool for the Kingdom of God? Hint: it wasn't the latter option.

Now, don't get me wrong. I love helping people. I know the things I've learned about marketing don't seem like common sense to some. I know the skills I've acquired over the years have taken just that—years—to develop. When people seek out my time and expertise, I want to help them. I enjoy what I do, and I want to be able to help educate people so they, too, can carry out similar responsibilities.

I've come to realize, while I do enjoy it and want to help everyone I can, it just isn't a realistic thing to do. If I devote my time and energy outside of normal work hours to others who also want to spend a chunk of time with me, then what time and energy will I have left to devote to creativity and writing, what I know I was created to do? Not a whole lot.

When I started from the beginning of Colossians and read in chapter one, "For in him all things were created: things in heaven and on earth, visible and invisible, whether thrones or powers or rulers or authorities; all things have been created through him and for him" (Colossians 1:16, NIV), it was like a wakeup call. I was reminded we were created through Him and for Him. It felt like a kick to the chest. I'd become so concerned with striving to strengthen my status among others, I'd let my priorities shift to running around doing everything for everyone, very similar to the story of Mary and Martha.

As Jesus and his disciples were on their way, he came to a village where a woman named Martha opened her home to him. She had a sister called Mary, who sat at the Lord's feet listening to what he said. But Martha was distracted by all the preparations that had to be made. She came to him and asked, "Lord, don't you care that my sister has left me to do the work by myself? Tell her to help me!"

"Martha, Martha," the Lord answered, "you are worried and upset about many things, but few things are needed— or indeed only one. Mary has chosen what is better, and it will not be taken away from her."
Luke 10:38-42, NIV

Jesus wasn't worried about what Martha was doing for Him; He wanted her present. He wasn't requiring the hustle; instead, he was encouraging the halt, and that meant taking time to sit at His feet.

How often do you take time to halt? Sometimes, it's easy to say yes after yes to requests that will increase your status in the eyes of others and bring in some extra money. Perhaps saying yes to tasks or events that will make you look good to your colleagues or family members is a no-brainer for you. It's easy to veer off your path and into the paths of others; especially when the things you are being called to do might not bring an immediate income, or even an income at all. What I've come to learn is that it doesn't matter. Whether your plans lead to a couple extra dollars, a couple of hundred dollars, or zero dollars, the value doesn't matter. When you pursue and do the things you were created to do, blessings fall.

The Lord provides in ways you do not expect or imagine. The reward may be physical, spiritual, or emotional. When you take the steps the Lord is nudging you to take, big things happen, and He moves in ways unexplainable to the human mind. You're holding my book in your hand, so you already know I took the steps to chase down the dream He laid on my heart years ago.

I took advantage of a fluctuating work schedule to devote

more time to writing, rather than attending to the needs of others. I feel guilty about saying "no" sometimes. That's the time I have to remind myself who I'm living for. Am I striving to live for and please others, or am I living for Jesus?

Have I been given this season to spread myself thin and tend to every request of those around me, or can I take a step back and take time to intentionally pursue the passions in my heart?

Let me tell you a little story about how this book came to life.

For a year and a half, I had a fifty-minute commute to work each day, one way. I would drive the first twelve miles to the highway in silence, using the time for prayer. That stretch of highway, surrounded by corn and bean fields, became my space of intention, a time when my sole focus was on conversation with the Lord. It was in the quietness where He would speak to me.

One day, I didn't feel like turning on any music, so I just kept driving in silence. I had a lot on my mind with work and what my next steps would be, so I spent some time praying about it. I can remember the spot right outside of Bradford, about twenty-five minutes from where I live, when the words "Break the Chains" popped into my head. Three simple words.

I'd been praying about writing and speaking opportunities. Not long after that is when those words came into my mind. What could that mean for me? What did my life have to do with breaking the chains? Could I somehow use them to bring glory to God through my life? What would that look like?

As I drove and thought about it, I began to feel peace, confidence, and direction that God wanted me to write about "breaking chains." He laid so heavily on my heart that we are all held by different chains that prevent us from living the life God created us to live. I've overcome or am working to overcome a chunk of those and know that those seasons of life weren't to be wasted.

Marrying Freedom

He carried me through those seasons, some kicking and screaming, some being pulled along, and some crawling at a turtle's pace. I know, for certain, I wouldn't have made it through without His strength, peace, and joy. I knew the pain that life could bring, but I had come to know and believe that the Lord was bigger than all of it and would carry me through whatever came my way. He didn't want me to keep all that I'd learned to myself. Sure, I am a quiet and private person, and it would stretch me out of my comfort zone to be vulnerable. However, He wanted to use me to show others that they too could have the same freedom and joyful abundance I now live in.

When I had about five minutes left in my drive, I turned on the radio. Guess what song began to play? "Chain Breaker" by Zach Williams.

Hello, Lord. I've got you. The seed was planted, and now, you're holding the fruit.

Whether you feel the Lord's been nudging you to take a new job, move to a new city, pursue a different degree, change careers, start a business, or establish a friendship with someone you never imagined, the possibilities are endless. It might be an easy decision for you to make, or it could seem like something you'd have no idea how to navigate.

I encourage you to take the step, whatever it is. Don't try to run full force ahead; instead, focus on small, actionable steps you can take each day. You don't have to have it all figured out right when you start. Instead, step into it, day to day. You might not know how, but God will show you the way. You may have lived your entire life, up until now, striving to live for someone else and have no idea what it would look like not to have that hold on your life anymore. It could terrify you to think of not living for that individual or thing any longer.

Let today be the day you learn how that feels. Let it be the day you begin to thrive in being who God created you to be. Don't be discouraged if your progress doesn't happen instantaneously. It could take you a few attempts to break free. Some of you have been living in it for so long, it might take some extensive time and effort. It will take baby steps and learning how to say "no" to requests that occupy your time, but don't fill your heart.

Even as I wrote this book, I went through seasons of complete dedication and then abandonment. There were moments of happiness and days when tears wouldn't stop falling. It took a complete, hard reevaluation of who I was and where I was going, but the Lord remained faithful through it all.

Show yourself some grace. Do not become frustrated if you mess up or slip back into your old habits, at times. I'm telling you now because I've slipped, veered, taken the wrong exit, pursued the wrong things, and tried to do it all on my own. It has been a messy journey, but He has remained faithful and always led me back to Him. If you knew how many times I got so excited and full-force ahead with writing this book, then became distracted and unmotivated, you would understand. You have to know right now, the Devil will try to call you back to your old way of living. He knows when you are about to do something amazing for the Lord, so he will do whatever he can think of to sway you back toward him. Don't ever forget God is always there. No matter how many times you prioritize something or someone above Him, He will be right there with open arms.

So, how do you start? Try this: do not fill your schedule with things you think will make you look "good." Instead, fill it with the things that set your soul on fire. Fill your soul instead of striving for status.

When you keep stepping and keep learning little by little how to do it, and how to go from living for others to living for the Lord, there will be a shift. It might seem like too small steps that you are taking, but they're not. Little habits, day after day, will continue to build. Those repeated actions will compound, and soon, you will notice they have turned into big results. Remain committed to consistency! The efforts will grow and the momentum will begin to increase, so don't be discouraged if you feel like your beginning is too small. Don't compare your page one to someone else's page seventy. It will become easier. Someday soon, you'll look back and see the insane growth, and you'll be so grateful you never gave up.

Be still and open to the possibilities. Remember, Mary took the time to sit at Jesus' feet, and that made all of the difference. He offers a life that is more than just items on a to-do list. He offers a life full of joy, laughter, peace, and love, and it's just on the other side of trusting Him with your free time as well as your schedule and plans.

<u>Uncap the Pen:</u>

When you get out of bed in the morning, what do your first thoughts involve? Do they drift to the tasks and responsibilities others have laid on you or that you've involved yourself in, or does it wander to the possibilities the day might bring? Explain.

____

____

____

____

Filling Your Soul Instead of Striving for Status

Who or what is one task, friend, family member, or colleague that you need to start saying "no" to, knowing that when you fulfill any obligations for that situation, it drains you and does not bring joy or passion into your life?

____

____

____

Take five minutes to sit at Jesus' feet. No cell phone. No computer. No books. No distractions. Just you. Close your eyes and breathe. Was it hard? Do you feel less stressed? Are you thinking more clearly? Write down how you feel after doing this. I encourage you to do this at least once a day!

____

____

____

Name one thing you can do in your day today that will help you break free. Could you block out time to serve, pursue your passions, pray, read, spend time catching up with a friend? Pick one thing that you will do, and try to incorporate it each day this week. If you miss it or mess up, do not give up or get discouraged. Just don't miss two days in a row. Pick back up where you left off. It will become an integral part of your day before you know it.

____

____

____

<u>Sign the Divorce Papers:</u>

"Father, there is nothing I want more than to live a life devoted to You. I know Your plans and blessings are far more abundant than I can even dream. I am well aware of this, but I still struggle with prioritizing the life You want me to lead. I strive to climb the ranks and achieve the highest status in the eyes of those around me more than I desire You. Shift my focus back to You, God. Where You are, there is life and peace overflowing. I want to thrive with You and for You. I want to carve time out of my days to live for You and not let my schedule or tasks prevent me from doing so. Help me to discern what I should say no to and how I can realign my schedule to make it more efficient and productive in Your name. Let every yes be for You and You alone."

Alleviating Your Anxiety

*The angel of the Lord encamps around those who fear
him, and he delivers them.*
Psalm 34:7, NIV

"You have anxiety. You'll need to be put on anxiety medication
and see a counselor."

As a fifth grader, these were words I never expected to hear.

I had been feeling off. I felt sick to my stomach often. If I were
in a crowd full of people, I'd make sure I knew where the
nearest exit was. If we were staying overnight somewhere, I
found comfort in knowing there was a hospital nearby. I can't
tell you why my thoughts would wander there, or why I was
so worried about things I couldn't control at such a young
age.

I don't remember how long I received counseling or the
length of time I was on the anxiety medication, but I do
remember, after a while, I was okay again. For quite a few
years, things were fine.

If I remember right, I was okay until college. Senior year,
second semester . . . final exams, to be exact. Sounds like the
perfect time to have an anxiety spell, *right*? I was taking my
Astronomy final. It was not only my last final of the semester
but also my very last day of college. While I tried to answer
the questions, I couldn't sit still for the life of me. It became
hard for me to concentrate. I made it through the exam, but
there were times I didn't think I would.

Once graduation was over, it went away for a bit. I ventured off
to the East Coast and worked, then bounced around to a few
other gigs over the next year and a half. I was driving and flying
by myself either daily or weekly, so I'd get anxious about that
every now and then. I didn't let it slow me down or stop me.

I kept my mind occupied with working and pushing through.

At the end of one of the contracts, I moved back home with my parents. At the time, some family friends were at the beginning stages of launching a new church about twenty-five minutes from us. I'd been attending a church that was almost an hour's drive each Sunday, so the thought of traveling twenty-five minutes was exciting to me. Even better, it took place in a barn on a Saturday night! Yes, a barn. If you're curious, we live out in the boonies in the middle of nowhere, so hearing of a church service that was being held in a barn sure piqued my interest. I soon became very involved and wanted to attend every event.

They hosted a women's Bible study that met every week, and there was also a Bible study beginning in my hometown at one of my favorite coffee shops. It was as if everything were falling into place. The things I'd longed for were now a reality.

I had a consistent and strong group of friends in college that met weekly for Bible study and worship, and with all of my traveling and bouncing around, I longed for another Christ-centered group to do life with.

For Godly women that I could learn from; People I could turn to and be vulnerable and open with.

The studies began, and I was loving it. I couldn't wait to attend every week. However, before long, the anxiety crept in. Sitting around a table for more than a few minutes seemed impossible in my mind.

The panicky feelings were back in full force, and this time, they seemed to occur at the places I longed to be—Bible study and church.

Why was I, all of a sudden, feeling overwhelmed with anxiousness at the place my heart desired to be, in a place where God was so present? I knew the enemy was rampant in that season of my life. When I finally had the very thing I'd been anticipating and praying for, it was as if he was using all of his tricks and ploys to keep me away and prevent me from going each week.

It happened every time I attended. The feelings would kick in. Bathroom break? Yes, please. I couldn't sit through the full session, and if I did, I couldn't sit still while I was there; I was crossing and uncrossing my legs, tapping my foot, antsy. I began counting down the time until I could leave and go back to the comforts of my home.

This was not who I was, and I knew it. This was not how I wanted to feel. This was not how Jesus wanted me to live. Every time those feelings overcame me, I got so angry.

"Lord, I want to be here. I want it more than anything, so why am I becoming so anxious?"

It was the same at church. Worship at the beginning of the service is my favorite part. However, it became a time when my palms were sweaty, and I'd consider going to the bathroom. Once we were sitting down and the pastor was giving his sermon, I was fine, but up until that point, it was a battle beneath the surface.

It reminded me of David fleeing from King Saul, except I was trying to flee the anxiety.

It didn't start out with David on the run from someone trying to kill him; it started when he ran towards what everyone else feared, the giant, Goliath.

Goliath started walking toward David again, and David ran quickly toward the Philistine battle line to fight him. He reached into his bag and took out a stone, which he slung at Goliath. It hit him on the forehead and broke his skull, and Goliath fell face downward on the ground. And so, without a sword, David defeated and killed Goliath with a sling and a stone!
1 Samuel 17:48-50, GNT

News about this victory spread, and soon the people were celebrating. "As they danced, they sang: "Saul has slain his thousands, and David his tens of thousands" (1 Samuel 18:7, NIV). Saul was angered and afraid of David because the Lord was with David and had departed from him. Saul made it his mission to kill David so he couldn't become king.

David knew Saul's plans and spent a solid portion of his life fleeing from him. There were times he narrowly escaped him. I can only imagine his constant state of anxiety. Though he came close to capture, the Lord protected David each and every time. Through all of the dodging and fleeing, David still authored Psalm 34, and declared this statement of trust that God would be his deliverer.

"I sought the Lord, and he answered me; he delivered me from all my fears. Those who look to him are radiant; their faces are never covered with shame. This poor man called, and the Lord heard him; he saved him out of all his troubles. The angel of the Lord encamps around those who fear him, and he delivers them."
Psalm 34:4-7, NIV

Just as the Lord answered David, I knew He would do the same for me. I'd gone in for my annual doctor's appointment that year and was talking to my doctor about it. She had one recommendation to help: anxiety medication. I hate taking medication of any kind, so that was the absolute last thing I wanted. I declined. If I was going to do this, it was going to have to be on my own and through the grace of God. He would be my deliverer.

My sister-in-law and I follow a few young adults on social media that have been role models to us. Carson Case moved from Myrtle Beach, to Charleston, and is now in Orlando, creating a community of young adults who are serving the Lord and stepping boldly into what He has for them. He's written a devotional called, *Born For It*, and is building a company called Bulletproof, that is full of personal development, accountability, and community with like-minded people. Noah Herrin led a church in Cleveland, TN, preached for a season in Georgia, and is now working to plant a church in Tennessee, with his wife. He also released a book called Viral Jesus. They're both younger than me. They're both resilient and passionate about serving the Lord. It brings my heart so much excitement to see people in our generation stepping up. I see what they're doing and am reminded that it is possible for any of us to serve right where we are, no matter our age.

We have been following their journeys for a few years and admire their passion and love for the Lord. They're all about leading our generation, and we're all for learning how to do the same where we are.

They announced they would be putting on a conference in February of 2018, so we decided in January we were not going to miss it. We bought our tickets a few weeks before and counted down the days until it arrived.

The conference was in Cleveland, Tennessee, so it was a ten-hour drive from where we lived. Yes, we're crazy enough to drive ten hours for a weekend conference. In the name of Jesus, let's go!

We loaded up the car and set off. Driving was another thing that had become a struggle for me, especially longer distances. I was nervous, to begin with, but I wasn't going to let that stand in my way of taking this trip. I would do whatever I could to surrender all of my nervousness and anxiety to the Lord.

Mile by mile, we were driving, farther away from the comforts of home and into a weekend that would change me forever.

I can tell you, in detail, how I felt that first night there. It was as it had been so many times before, but this time, something shifted. It was during worship when my hands started to sweat, and I mapped out the nearest exit to the bathroom to get away from the unfamiliar crowds, as I'd done so many times before. Safety. Comfort. Quiet.

NO. I will not.

Not this time. I prayed and pleaded with the Lord. I knew this anxiety wasn't coming from Him; I didn't drive ten hours to come to worship Him and spend time with Him, only to let the Devil win and make me bounce out during worship.

I wasn't going to. I couldn't let him continue to have this hold on me. Not today, Satan. Not again. Not ever.

After that, it was as if surrendering my struggle to God and worshiping through the anxiety allowed the Lord to give me the strength to overcome it. For the next two days, I didn't feel anxious, I didn't feel afraid, and I didn't get sweaty palms. I basked in the goodness and power of our Lord and knew He had helped me reach an important milestone in my journey.

Being surrounded by young adults worshiping the Lord together and hearing testimonies of His power in the lives of others was incredible. It was the first conference I had ever been to, and it was the most encouraging place that I'd ever been. I heard stories of His faithfulness and believed with my whole heart that He was and is faithful, and I trusted He would continue to show up through this season. He was bigger than my giant. He was helping me overcome it.

There was one song that never left me and still to this day hasn't: "Mighty Warrior" by David Virgo. (Stop right now, and listen to it! And while you're at it, you might as well listen to "You'll Bring Me Through," as well.) David is amazing and so talented, and his songs will speak to your situations.

I began declaring the promises in those songs over my anxiety, and little did I know, I would soon walk through a season of hardship where those lyrics became my anthem.

God knew. He knew I needed that conference to prepare me for the next few months of trials and difficulties. He knew that, through my time in Cleveland, I'd learn to keep stepping with Him and to trust Him to handle whatever I faced. I understood, in a new way, that He would be bigger than any of my giants, I just needed to surrender it all to Him. He would help alleviate those anxious feelings I was experiencing.

Now, I won't lie and tell you I was healed from my anxiety that weekend, never to experience it again. Yes, I felt calmer at church and didn't want to dart for the door. Driving became bearable, and, just a few months later, I was commuting two hours a day without any issues.

There are still times when I do experience it, though not to the extent that it once was. Now, when I feel those anxious thoughts creep in, I turn to the Lord. I knew, through worshiping Him, He had helped me overcome it once, and He would continue to do it again until I could walk through any circumstance without anxiety peeping in. I pray, repeat His truths, and fill my mind with His promises until the anxiety subsides.

Cast all your anxiety on him because he cares for you.
1 Peter 5:7, NIV

"Therefore I tell you, do not worry about your life, what you will eat or drink; or about your body, what you will wear. Is not life more than food, and the body more than clothes"
Matthew 6:25, NIV

What you focus on will consume you. If you focus your thoughts on your calm center, on God's truths, on breathing in and out, letting those thoughts drift away as clouds in the sky, you'll realize that, like the clouds, those feelings of anxiety and the overwhelming sense of panic will pass.

Remember, there is nothing you will ever face that the Lord doesn't already know is coming. There is nothing you will struggle with that the Lord hasn't experienced, and nothing will take Him by surprise. Whatever it is, it will never be too big or too much for Him. Your anxiety might be high, and you may not be able to remember what life was like without it, but don't let the enemy deceive you into believing you have to stay there or that you deserve to live that way.

Don't let him trick you into giving up. You've got this, and the Lord is right beside you to fight your battle.

I'm not a doctor, nor am I certain that prayer and worship will indeed cure your long-fought battle with anxiety. This is not a topic that has a one-size fits all solution. It will look different for everyone. What I've shared is what has helped me. This is how I've fought my battles. When I focus on Him, I find that peaceful center again. I seek Him, pursue Him, pray to Him, and trust in Him to deliver me from anything contrary to what He wants for me.

Maybe, for you, it looks a little different. What are some things that can clear your mind and ease your anxiety? For you, it might look like meditating, doing yoga, talking to a friend, going for a walk, or practicing mindfulness. Some may need professional help or medications, and that's okay; there is nothing at all wrong with that. I've been to a counselor, and I'm not ashamed to say that. They are professionals, and they are trained in how to help an individual deal with anxiety. I know many people who go to a counselor on a regular basis, whether for anxiety or self maintenance. I'll say it again, just so you grasp it: **there is nothing wrong with seeking help**. I even encourage it. It never hurts to get to know yourself better. You may uncover things you don't realize are affecting you—things you need to heal and mend before you can break free.

Flip the cards. Make the Devil the anxious one, anxious about the power of God in your life. Make him fret that he no longer has a hold on you. You have a mighty warrior on your side, and He is declaring victory over your life.

Uncap the Pen:

Have you ever experienced an anxiety attack? Not being able to breathe, palms sweaty, panicky feelings? Maybe you didn't experience those symptoms but reflect on a moment when you felt extreme anxiety. What were you thinking? How did you feel?

____

____

____

What did you do, or what do you do, to calm yourself when anxious feelings arise?

____

____

____

What is one thing that seems to always make you anxious, whether it be a thought, an action, a person, or a place? Uncover it now and become more aware of what triggers you. Next time you face this circumstance, make a conscious effort to find your calm center.

____

____

____

Now, write a few affirmations and truths you will focus on when anxiety strikes. Let the Lord be bigger than your anxieties. Cast your thoughts on Him. He's got you.

____

____

____

____

____

____

<u>Sign the Divorce Papers:</u>

"God, when my mind wanders and is overcome with anxious thoughts, lead me back to calm waters. Renew me. Be my anchor in the storm, my peace in the waves. Lord, I know anxiety does not come from You. I'm aware the enemy will use any tactics he can to try to overtake me. I know You are bigger than all of it. Help me believe You can lift me, You can deliver me. Show me the people You created who can help me through this season and overcome the anxious thoughts. I know You are bigger than anything I will ever face. Help me truly believe and walk in that freedom with every ounce of who I am. Guide my steps, my thoughts, and anything that enters into my mind. You're my peace, and You're all I need."

Facing Your Fears

The Lord is my light and my salvation—whom shall I fear?
The Lord is the stronghold of my life—of whom
shall I be afraid?
Psalm 27:1, NIV

The unknown.
Failing.
Disappointing others.
Not being good enough.
Loving.
Losing.

There are many things that can evoke fear each day. Some of you are paralyzed and unable to go past your current level of comfort because you're terrified of exploring what's in the depths of the unknown.

Friend, you weren't created to be stuck. The Lord wants you to walk in peace, happiness, and freedom. You may believe His thoughts and ways are the best, yet fear holds you in your current state. You have doubts and believe you will mess up. Some of you fear that if you commit to following Jesus and what He's laid on your heart, He will ask too much. You fear you will do too little or that you'll never measure up. You feel as if someone else could do it better and that even though you thought you were, you're not the one for the job. You can't live like this any longer!

He will never bring you to something that will be too much for you. He will never make you do something you aren't ready for, that He hasn't somehow already prepared you for. He wants to take you where you think you cannot go. He knows you can go even farther.

He created the mountains, the stars, and everything we see. He brought the dead bones to life. He can do a work beyond our imaginations in our lives if we take a step in obedience and trust He will move.

Let me tell you a little story about a time when fear consumed my entire heart, mind, and soul. I had a meeting scheduled at work that was over two weeks out, and I was so afraid to have it. In the weeks leading up to it, it was all I could think about, from the moment my eyes opened in the morning until the time I drifted off to sleep. However, the sleep was fleeting. I'd toss and turn, unable to shake the fear of this conversation I knew was coming and didn't want to face.

The thing is, it wasn't a meeting I needed to stress about, but I did. It was supposed to be a discussion about my future and my salary at the organization, but I already knew I was planning to submit my resignation. I felt the Lord calling me away from my time there, and I was afraid of disappointing and letting someone I cared about down. The very thought of sharing my heart with him terrified me.

I knew I didn't need to worry, and I trusted with my whole heart that the Lord had it under control. I had learned, over the years, whatever situations I go through, if and when the Lord is in them, there's no reason to fear. I was reassured and remembered He promises us peace in His word: "Peace I leave with you; my peace I give you. I do not give to you as the world gives. Do not let your hearts be troubled and do not be afraid" (John 14:27, NIV).

If I knew all of that and "believed it," then why was I so afraid? I wish I could tell you, but instead, I let the enemy in my ear, taunting me, telling me I needed to be fearful about this conversation.

Let's fast forward through those long, agonizing weeks to the night before the meeting. How much do you think I slept that night, knowing God had it under control and it would all be fine? Like a baby? Nope. It was as if I'd just birthed a newborn baby that woke up every hour because the sleep was so sporadic.

Facing Your Fears

How could I claim I was trusting the Lord with my whole heart yet let this meeting get to me so much? Well, folks, we're all human. I'm great at believing for others, encouraging and reassuring them of God's plan for their lives and reminding them of His faithfulness. But when it comes to walking through it for myself . . . It's a work in progress. I'm a work in progress, day in and day out, and I'm not ashamed of that. Just because I'm sharing these insights with you doesn't mean I've perfected it, because I'm still handing it over to the Lord and working on it every single day.

Alas, the day arrived. Oh, but you haven't even heard the best part yet! The meeting I'd stressed about for weeks? It got RESCHEDULED. Not just for a few hours or until the next day. Nope. Rescheduled for WEEKS later.

There was no way I'd make it through a few more weeks; unless, of course, I wanted to lose my mind. I didn't like how high-strung and anxious I'd become. I knew I was not stepping on the path that God created for me, and now that this meeting was delayed, I was going to either have to initiate the conversation about it myself or let it simmer and continue living like this. The longer I waited, the less obedient I would be, and the more out of alignment I would feel in my walk with the Lord.

It reminded me of Gideon. The Lord called him to lead Israel out of Midian's hand. He came up with excuse after excuse.

"Pardon me, my lord," Gideon replied, "but if the Lord is with us, why has all this happened to us? Where are all his wonders that our ancestors told us about when they said, 'Did not the Lord bring us up out of Egypt?' But now the Lord has abandoned us and given us into the hand of Midian."

The Lord turned to him and said, "Go in the strength you have and save Israel out of Midian's hand. Am I not sending you?"

"Pardon me, my lord," Gideon replied, "but how can I save

Marrying Freedom

Israel? My clan is the weakest in Manasseh, and I am the least in my family."

The Lord answered, "I will be with you, and you will strike down all the Midianites, leaving none alive."
Judges 6:13-16, NIV

The Lord told him, word for word, He would be with him. It didn't matter how weak or strong he felt, or that he was the least in his family, the Lord would help him defeat the clan. Gideon didn't take God at His word, though. He asked for confirmation not once, but three separate times. He wanted to be 110% sure he would be protected. He was afraid to take the leap and trust God, but when he did, the Israelites, who had been oppressed for years, were freed. They didn't wait for this freedom for a year or two. It took seven years of oppression. They were released when Gideon took God at His word.

I knew this would be a similar situation. The Lord laid it on my heart, more than once, that it was time to move on from my current role, and I knew this was a time when He was going to challenge me to speak up and trust Him. Cue more fear. I am more of an introvert who doesn't like to initiate challenging conversations, but I was prompted to do so. It was time for me to go for it. I knew if I didn't, if I continued living in the mindset I had in that season, I'd be in misery.

The next day, the opportunity arose. It was time. My hands were shaking as I sat with my boss, and we chatted about a few different things. Then, the perfect transition. It was now or never.

Guess what the Lord did? He guided each word, and I felt so much peace during and after.

On my drive home, my sister called, and we were replaying everything. She asked if I cried during the conversation, because I can be an emotional person. To her surprise and mine, the response was, "No." Tears didn't fall. I didn't even feel a tiny inclination to cry or be afraid.

On the hour commute, though, tears did want to flow. I was so overwhelmed with relief and with how good God is, how He can bring such peace to any and every situation, when we step into what He's asking us to do.

There is no reason to be fearful. When you feel as if the Lord is nudging you to do something, and you don't do it, you're being disobedient to Him. Sure, things may work out eventually, but you might be prolonging the process by not doing what you know you're called to do.

I've been there. I've had it in my heart to write for years. There have been many instances that have confirmed this is something I was born to do. However, when given the opportunity and the "extra" time that I could use to write, I fell into the trap of pleasing people and finding excuse after excuse to focus on other things.

I could use this time to write, but I have to get this post done for this business.

I want to finish writing this chapter, but it's so nice outside, and winter will be coming, so I'd better go for a walk instead.

I have an extra thirty minutes before work, but I think I'll scroll my Instagram feed and see what everyone else is up to right now. Maybe doing so will inspire me to get to work.

Did it ever work that way? Nope.

I've read a ton of books myself, and I've always wanted to publish one. I've talked about doing it for years.

What was stopping me then? Fear.

Fear no one would want to read it.

Fear I would spend all of this time creating, writing, editing, and digging into the depths of my soul for past experiences and how to relate to others, only to have no way for others to see it.

Fear I wouldn't be able to get it published. How does one even go about approaching publishers as a new author?

Fear of what people would think after reading the pages. Would they look at me differently? Would they like it? Would they criticize it? Would they think I was silly? Would they be able to relate to my words?

Fear.

You're holding this in your hand right now, but you need to know I was afraid; I was "jumping out of an airplane" type afraid. I created excuse after excuse and prolonged the process way longer than I would like to admit. Through a Bible study of the book of Revelation at my church and my first twenty-one-day fast, I knew I couldn't wait any longer. The Lord spoke to me louder than ever that it was time to write.

In our study of Revelation, the Revelation of Jesus and the things yet to come was a heavy emphasis. We learned more about what it will be like leading up to His second coming. We don't know when Jesus is coming, but there's no time to waste. If we take a look at the world around us, I think it's easy to say we need to live with urgency, carrying out things that will glorify God and His Kingdom, that could show others who He is and how much He loves us. After that study, I couldn't write this book fast enough. I didn't just desire to write it; I needed to write it. I needed those who read it to know who Jesus is. More than anything, I want to have everyone around me in heaven when it's time for us to leave this earth, and not only those in my sphere but those I don't even know, those I will never even meet.

I'm sure you and I have been through similar life experiences, and, in reading some of my stories, you can put yourself in my shoes and feel the emotions I felt. However, our talents may be very different from one another. Regardless, "We are God's handiwork, created in Christ Jesus to do good works, which God prepared in advance for us to do" (Ephesians 2:10, NIV). He crafted each of us with a unique purpose. He knows He can use me through my words. When I share articles, write posts, and publish books, they will act as vessels that allow others to see and hear about Jesus. He helps make the words relatable so others can put themselves in my shoes and learn who He is through them. He knows that through the content I share, He will have the means to reach someone and remind them they can find new hope, even though their situation may seem impossible. It could look similar for you. Perhaps, you too, are a passionate writer or your purpose could be something I'll never try or experience. Step into it!

When you're walking that path and you come across something that incites fear, I want you to remember something: The circumstances might look different than the stories I share in this book, but remember the pattern in each chapter. God was faithful in every single season, time and time again. Trust, and believe that for your journey. Have confidence in the fact that when you take a leap and trust Him with the details, whatever those might look like, He will move and prove faithful in your life, too.

Sometimes we go through situations that are similar to those around us. When we realize we're not alone in our struggles, we don't feel as overwhelmed with the fears that have taken root in our lives. Instead of focusing on defeat, we discover we can help one another overcome them.

The Lord knew from the beginning of time that when I surrendered my time and talents to Him, I'd help tell the story of how He changed my life and how He's broken away so many chains that inhibited my freedom. He wants to help you do the same, to give you the pen and paper to sign your name on the dotted line there, on the final divorce paper. It's time for you to live freely, too!

Marrying Freedom

The best part of stepping out in faith, even if there's a tiny bit of fear, is knowing the Lord is and will be glorified through it. He will give you everything you need to work through and overcome, and He will accomplish great things through you. Many times, you will look back, and see what you overcame. You will see how it all came together, piece by piece. Many times, in that reflection, you realize only God could have done it. Just as the Israelites were freed when Gideon took the leap, lives will be changed when you step into who you were created to be—people will break free from the chains of fear that have been locked on them for days, months, and for some, years.

Even as I've sat down to write through these topics, it has continued to challenge and change me from the inside out. It's taken constant surrender. I haven't thought through some of these topics for a while. Cue the fear of digging deeper into my subconscious. What will I uncover? Some of the lessons I viewed with a fresh perspective. So much time has passed since I thought about them. Cue the enemy reminding me of the pain and attempting to lure me back into feelings of bitterness, regret, or unforgiveness. Some I've been able to view with more grace, peace, and hope, no matter how fresh or old wounds might be. Cue the devil's faint whispers, "You can't forgive that. You don't deserve good. No one wants to read about that." He's put in my mind the fear of sharing the wrong thing, the wrong way . . . fear, fear, fear, creeping in my ear.

Through this writing process, I've learned to surrender it and let Him help me work through it instead of avoiding, masking, and hiding.

When you sit down and dig deeper into what you're afraid of and, like me, sit down to have that conversation you've been anticipating, are you going to lean into it with faith, or are you going to launch as far away as you can to avoid the thing you've been fearing?

Don't delay, and don't anticipate it with dread. Face it head-on, one step at a time, and watch the enemy cower in fear at the power the Lord will give you over the lies. You, acting on the things you were created to do, WILL scare the Devil and make him nervous. There's nothing he hates more than to see someone stepping out in faith to fulfill their God-honoring future. Oh man; it scares the daylights out of him. His tactics to distract you will escalate, so be prepared to face opposition but have no fear. He knows you are going to do something big, so do it! You don't have to have it all figured out on day one. Just start. The Devil is the one that is scared now, as he should be!

God isn't like humans. He doesn't get distracted or have things come up to interrupt plans. No; He isn't going to reschedule your appointment like humans often do. He's got it on His calendar, not in pencil, but in a permanent pen, and He's going to keep it. When you walk in step with Him and honor Him, He will bring you to it, through it, and use it to bring His Kingdom glory. He will give you everything you need to stand tall over unbelief. It's time to stop living in fear and launch into the confident, bold life He designed you to live. Don't be afraid. There is no time to waste. The time is now.

Uncap the Pen:

Take a few minutes and create a list of things that create a sense of fear inside of you.

____

____

____

____

Now, take some time to think through those particular fears. What causes you to be fearful about each one? Whether it's something rational or something completely irrational, try to determine where the fear is coming from.

____

____

____

____

What truths do you need to stand on when the Devil tries to overcome you with those fears?

____

____

____

Name a time when you acted even when you were afraid and you saw God show up in a big way. Were you expecting Him to show up, or was it more of a surprise? How do you feel when you remember His faithfulness in this instance? Describe the circumstance and your reaction.

____

____

____

____

<u>Sign the Divorce Papers:</u>

"Lord, I know that fear is not of You. There is no reason to be fearful. Give me the strength to stand tall over my fears and conquer them. I know You are bigger than anything and everything I will ever face, every mountain and every valley. Your glory will prevail through any and every instance. Give me faith to believe it and step in confidence, in boldness, in trust. There will be times I doubt; there will be times I am so afraid to take that first step. Help me put one foot in front of the other, until I am running the race You have set before me. Be bigger than any fear, and be the biggest thing in my life. I know You tower over the details of my days. I want to be confident in You, even when I'm full of fear. Help me truly believe You've got this."

Canceling the Comparison

Do not conform to the pattern of this world, but be transformed by the renewing of your mind. Then you will be able to test and approve what God's will is—his good, pleasing and perfect will.
Romans 12:2, NIV

When I was growing up, AOL Instant Messenger was THE thing to have. It was the place where we could sign on and talk to our friends. We didn't text each other, because that wasn't a thing yet. Instead, we'd call each other on the landlines, then wait for our dial-up internet to load so we could log on and message one another all night long.

The way we lived growing up was so different from today. If you ask a fifteen-year-old if their house has a landline, they probably wouldn't even know what that means. Children now grow up with cell phones, unlimited text and minutes, and social media. People, more often than not, have their heads down on their phones.

One bitter-cold Saturday, I went out to lunch with my friend. There was a short wait, and the place was packed full of people. Once we were seated, we looked around to see how many people were there.

Do you know what we observed? A restaurant, full of people, who may have spent the morning in anticipation of lunch together with their loved ones, friends, or family, excited for their schedules to finally align so they could catch up.

What we saw didn't portray that anticipation. There were tables of people talking, but at nearly every table, the guests were glancing at their phones every few seconds, half engaged with the people in front of them and more concerned with what was at their fingertips. Could it be that they were posting about where they were and who they were with, then scrolling to see what was going on in the lives of their "friends"?

We began talking about social media and our generation, how sad it is that everyone is out and about, yet so consumed with their phones, they're not truly present. The sad thing is, it's not just in public. It's at home, school, and work. People are there in the flesh, yet lack the attention span to pay attention to one another because technology consumes the moment.

Does this sound like you? Are you consumed with what others are doing, who they're with, what announcements are being posted, and doing so at the expense of time with family and friends? Rather than savor the moment, how often do you succumb to the scroll? How much are you missing out on?

Take a moment to reflect on yourself. When's the last time you went somewhere, or spent time with a good friend or family member, and didn't glance at your phone at least one time? It's okay if you can't answer, because I bet a lot of us can't recall our last uninterrupted, fully-attentive conversation.

During the season of COVID and quarantines, restrictions, and limits on gatherings, it's probably safe to say many of us would have given anything to go out to eat with our loved ones without the worry of masks and social distancing. We yearned for some sort of normalcy. Now that many establishments have lessened the strict rules, I wonder if you are still quick to get on your phone when out with family or friends? Or, do you appreciate the moments of gathering more than you did before? Do you soak up every moment spent with others outside of your household? Or do you take those moments for granted, living as if isolation will never be required again?

Even before quarantine, it was so easy to become absorbed by scrolling through social media. We scroll as we sit at a stoplight, turn to it when we wake in the morning, and get on it when we're at our friend's house and there's a pause in conversation. Many of us have been at home more than ever, and our scrolling has increased; it's as if we can't take a break from it. We experience FOMO (Fear of Missing Out) and end up missing out on our lives because of it.

You see someone on vacation, another with a new item you want. You see an engagement announcement, a marriage announcement, or someone is having a baby. One lady is sharing her latest outfit haul, and another person just purchased a new car. A gentleman you know just got a promotion; your other friend just retired.

At this point, everyone shares everything, good or bad. Some have genuine intentions and post because it's an easy way to share their announcement with family and friends. Others post because they want attention or some sort of reaction from people. Some even share with ill intentions; they hope to make someone envious or they post out of spite and bitterness. Yes, social media can be a beautiful thing, but it can also use you, and the downfalls far outweigh the benefits.

When did we become so focused on the applause of others that we forget who we're alive in and created to live for? Rather than an audience of One, we're focused on living a life full of fun, projecting a certain image to our "friends" that will make them think higher of us and maybe even envy us. Many of the friends we crave approval from are people whom we spend zero time with; some whom we have never met. We obsess over gaining their approval, getting the "likes," hoping for a "share" or "save," but, the funny thing is, those "followers" aren't thinking of us as much as we think they are. We live in a self-absorbed culture.

When you post, do you have a particular person in mind that you hope sees it? Do you think they are just sitting around, waiting for you to share something? Chances are, they are not.

What does this obsession with social media do to us, our

self-esteem, and our perspectives on our lives?

We begin to devalue ourselves and who we are because we let our everyday moments—the sad, the messy, the trivial, and boring—get caught up in the highlight reels of those online. We start to envy others. We become obsessed with having what "that person" has. We forget that those we are fangirling over on our screens also have a story and a journey. Though it seems they have it all together, what they share online is not all of who they are.

We skip over the fact that these people also have insecurities, struggles, pains, and difficulties. We forget they have real lives, just like us. They have mundane moments. They cry, they get nervous, they wake up and go to sleep each night. It appears they are living "the life," but their lives are no different than yours and mine, and we have no idea what that individual has gone through to get to where he or she is.

They just purchased a new car . . . But maybe they had to work more than seventy hours a week just to be able to afford it. Or maybe they're in debt up to their eyeballs, but they want to uphold the appearance they project to everyone, so they go farther and farther into debt. They'll never be able to retire because of that image they "need" to maintain.

They are on vacation somewhere beautiful . . . But maybe they haven't been on a vacation together in eight years, or maybe that vacation is the one time of year that the husband and wife spend together when they aren't bickering and on different schedules. You wouldn't believe what they had to do and sacrifice to be able to save the funds to go.

She works from home. . .But she doesn't know when to draw the line or how to take a break, so work eats up almost all of her waking hours. She can't recall the last time she took a break in the evening to have a true, honest conversation with her husband.

They seem like the happiest and sweetest couple . . . But

they struggle with insecurities and problems, just like the world around them.

She owns five different businesses . . . But she must sacrifice the kids' sporting events and birthday parties and so much time with her family and friends, just to keep the businesses profitable and running.

Do we want to live with hardened hearts, envious and bitter, because we "lack" what we see others have on social media? We can learn from the story of two sisters, Leah and Rachel, in Genesis 29. Leah was able to have children, but Rachel wasn't. There was nothing Rachel wanted more than to have some kiddos, and she became frustrated because God had given her sister children but not her.

A man named Jacob had married Leah, not because he loved her, but because he was tricked into it by her father. His heart loved and desired to be with Rachel, Leah's sister. When the Lord saw that Leah was not loved, he enabled her to conceive, but Rachel remained childless.
Genesis 29:31, NIV

Each was envious of the other because of what they had: Leah had the children, and Rachel was loved by Jacob, though he was also married to Leah. Each became more and more resentful as they compared and began to define themselves by what was lacking.

When Leah conceived her first three children, she'd hoped her husband would fall more in love and choose her because she had borne him three sons; however, when the fourth was born, she said, "This time I will praise the Lord" (Genesis 29:31, NIV). She shifted her perspective and found her identity in God, instead of her husband. She stopped comparing herself to her sister and found contentment in how things were. And do you know what happened with that fourth son?! She named the child Judah, whose family line would one day lead to the birth of Jesus.

Marrying Freedom

Do you see what can happen when we realize where we are is where we need to be and we have everything we need? What happens when we shift from grumbling to grateful; when we stop comparing our lives to those around us and online, and we embrace the present moment, realities, and circumstances we're in? God can move and do amazing work, as He did with Leah. He brought the Messianic line from her. Just think of all of the possibilities and ways in which He could use you!

God created us, each with special talents, capabilities, passions, desires, and characteristics. Some of us are strong speakers, some are strong writers, and others make an impact through coaching, serving those in need, caring for the ill, or teaching. Some of us will have children and families; others will not. We each have traits and journeys that make us who we are.

Just because someone can do something you can't doesn't make you any less valuable. Don't become consumed with the notion that because one account has more followers and gets more likes than you means they're more put together and better off than you. That is so far from the truth.

Comparison has become a pandemic for children as well. It breaks my heart to see them so consumed by their devices, to hear conversations of children sharing their insecurities, their "flaws," their discouragement and disappointment about how "popular" their latest TikTok was. I have three nieces who I adore, and sometimes when I listen to them talk, I just want to wrap them up and tell them how amazing they are because I can see and hear how much having social media has affected them—not to mention what social media is exposing them to.

Rather than allowing the social platforms to deem what's shareable, trending, or popular, we need to remind the people in our lives—the youth, our friends, family, and even ourselves, that they are enough, as they are. You, friend, are enough.

Canceling the Comparison

YOU are chosen. YOU are loved. YOU are enough. There are things you were created to do that God can accomplish through you alone. You do not have to change a single thing about who you are. Not now. Not ever. If someone tells you or makes you feel otherwise, that is a lie straight from the Devil.

Stop getting caught up in what everyone else is doing, and be present where you are. There are family members and friends around you, right now, that you probably miss so much quality time with because you're addicted to scrolling through your phone. Rather than sharing your latest updates with your "friends," share some quality time with those around you. There's no gift sweeter than being present.

You'll be surprised at how much happier you feel when you stop dwelling so much on what other people are doing and sharing and start appreciating where you are and who you're surrounded with. Each moment is a gift you should unwrap instead of remaining tied up in comparing every aspect of your life to others.

When 2019 started, one of my goals was not to check any of my personal social media accounts until noon. It was a little difficult, at first, because usually, I'd check it while I was working out in the morning or at the coffee shop before work. It got easier each day, and I found myself more excited to focus on more productive things. February came, and I was feeling weighed down with a few things going on. I felt the Lord was calling me to focus more of my attention on Him. He was urging me to use the time I would have spent on social media to read, journal, pray, or just be still.

Can I tell you something that brought me the biggest breath of fresh air? February came, and I deleted all of the social media apps on my phone for over a month. Yes, an entire month, and I'm still living and breathing. Instagram, Snapchat, and I never had the Facebook app on my phone; otherwise, that would've been gone too. Instead of scrolling through social media feeds, I found and continue to find myself opening my Bible app and completing different reading plans there. I even opened a physical book that would help me learn and grow.

Rather than focusing and being so absorbed and concerned with what others are doing, I have let the focus shift to my story and what God wants to use me for—not to pay much attention to the races other people are running, but instead, to stay in my lane, pursue the things He has laid on my heart, and be ready and open to be used, however He's directing my steps. By diving deeper into my relationship with and trust in Him, He showed me, day by day, that He had great plans in store. As I continued to seek Him, He made things clear that I was previously uncertain about, just like He will do for you.

How can you implement this practice into your life? Can you imagine what your morning would look like if, instead of grabbing your phone first thing, you grabbed His word? Instead of opening Facebook to see the latest media updates, welcoming the weight of the world into your bedroom or kitchen bright and early, what if you turned to a book to help you learn and grow? What if you stopped running to the rumblings of friends and strangers on your phone and became eager to elevate your mood by getting up and exercising? Perhaps you'd even use the time you spent scrolling to sit down with your spouse or a friend to have coffee?

What about the close of your day?
What would it look like if you shared the accomplishments and challenges of your day with your spouse or a trusted friend?
What if you journaled the good things and listed out some things you are grateful for each day?
What if you pursued ideas and activities that excited you, that energized you?
What if you did some physical activity that would help strengthen your body and decrease health issues in the long run, instead of perusing your phone for hours?
What if, instead of succumbing to the scroll, you strategize

Canceling the Comparison

for personal growth and success?

As a side gig, I promote a shampoo company. The team hosts weekly calls that focus on personal development. The leaders always talk about being 1% better every single day. It doesn't matter what the person next to us has done. Our focus should be solely on our own stories and being better versions of ourselves each day. I concentrate on applying that to my daily living. I can't compare my chapter three to someone else's chapter fifteen. I am where I am, and all I can do is work to learn, grow, and become a stronger version of myself, so I can continue being the person God created me to be. To do that, I put my blinders up. I stay focused on the road in front of me, instead of veering side-to-side trying to see what those alongside me are doing or have accomplished. It's time you put your blinders up as well. Let's protect our energy and our mindsets. Let's focus on developing ourselves a little bit more each day.

What are some easy steps you can take to get this started? Limit social media. Use it for what you need to, but don't allow it to use you any longer. It's been taking up too much of your time for far too long. If you find yourself addicted to it or as the first thing you turn to when you're bored, in an argument, or looking to pass the time, set a timer for yourself and stick to it. Put your phone or computer in the other room, where it's not easy for you to reach. Instead of your phone, pick up a personal development book. Listen to a podcast that will help you learn skills relevant to something you're passionate about. There are endless videos on YouTube you can look up and books you can order. If you aren't sure which leaders you should look up, a few of my favorites are Ed Mylett, Mel Robbins, John Maxwell, and Dean Graziosi. I've been recently reading The Power of Positive Thinking by Norman Vincent Peale; it has been a phenomenal read about mindset, and I highly recommend it!

We can spend our time dwelling on what we don't have, how many "likes" our recent post received, how we didn't get to go here or there like that person, or we can use our time living in the moment and commit to making the most of it, of stepping in obedience with Christ. We'll never be the person next to us, because that's not who we're called to be. We're called to be ourselves. Some of us will become a doctor, an influencer, a veterinarian, a stay-at-home mom, a business owner, and some of us won't. Whether you achieve those "dreamy titles" or not, you're still viewed by the Lord of all as if you are in a one-to-one meeting with Him. Imagine God as the CEO. You're the Senior Director. He can guide you, but only you can make the choices to step into all He's showing you. You have the opportunity to make the choices yourself. He won't make them for you.

He created you for a specific reason, and when you focus on Him, your vision will become a little clearer, your dream, a little more manageable. Small steps are all it takes. Small steps of obedience, of trust, of focusing on the path He laid before you. Small actionable steps taken day after day compound, and over time, those actions create big results. Just keep going. You are destined for great things. You are capable and strong. This unique journey is just beginning. Keep your eyes straight ahead, and don't get distracted by the things that will deter you. Don't get caught in the trap of comparison. Have a laser focus on the things you know He has for you, and you will feel a shift in your outlook on life. He has perfect timing and a perfect story, just for you. And guess what? It's a gift that's ready for you to unwrap. Untie the bow, and take the lid off the box. What's inside? I'll give you a hint: it's not the chains we talked about at the beginning of the book. It's 2,305,935x better.

Uncap the Pen:

What aspect of your life do you find yourself comparing to others? What provokes these feelings? Explain.

____

____

____

How easy is it to have a productive conversation while the person you're talking to is not fully engaged? Reflect on a time when either you or the person you were with were focused more on their device than on being present. How did you feel during that time?

____

____

____

Social media is great but can also cause one to feel insecure or insignificant. What is something you will do to replace scrolling on your phone? Is it talking with your spouse? Exercising? Reading? Journaling? Spending time with family or friends?

____

____

____

____

Challenge: Next time you're out to dinner or getting coffee with someone, or even just sitting at home with your family, have everyone at the table put their phones away and not take them out the entire time. When you've done this, explain the experience and what the ambiance at the table was like, minus phones to latch on to. Was it comfortable, or did people get uncomfortable not being able to glance at their phones?

____

____

____

____

____

<u>Sign the Divorce Papers:</u>

"Lord, thank You for creating me exactly as I am. I know I get caught up in comparing my life to those online, but I am very aware of the beautiful life You have blessed me with, of the people, places, and things that are a part of my life. It's easy to dwell on what I don't have after being on social media but fill my heart with thankfulness for this life. Life is beautiful, and I often take a lot of it for granted. Help me to live in gratitude and acceptance of what is, what was, and what will be. Take away the strong desire or sense of addiction I have to scroll. Replace it with thoughts of bettering myself and remembering how You see me. Stir in me a passion to pursue in place of that time spent comparing my journey to others. Social media is often the highlight reel of individuals; Help me to recognize when I begin to compare my in-betweens and transitions to those online. You made me who and how I am for a reason, and I'm grateful for each and every aspect of ME. Thank you, Jesus."

Revolutionizing Your Relationship Status

*You, my brothers and sisters, were called to be free. But do
not use your freedom to indulge the flesh; rather, serve one
another humbly in love.*
Galatians 5:13, NIV

"Do you have any children yet?
"Are you married?"
"Oh, do you have a boyfriend?"
"I know the perfect person to set you up with."

If I had a dollar for every time someone asked me those
questions, I'd be a millionaire a couple of times over, and
retired by now. It's unreal how many times I've been asked,
especially being in a position that involves communicating
and networking with a lot of different people each week.

Before I was married, and even before I was dating, I
contemplated buying one of those rubber wedding rings so
people would assume I was married and would stop asking
about my love life. If I was married, they'd leave me alone, right?

Each and every time I was asked one of those questions, it
took me down the same path every time: me, reflecting and
envisioning the romantic love story I planned to experience
by age twenty-five. It was a scene I had dreamed of in my
head thousands of times since I was a child. It didn't happen
when I expected it would. It came to pass at age twenty-
eight, three years past the age I anticipated.

I'm a huge Hallmark movie lover. They might be a tad cheesy,
but I love seeing two people persevere through the hard
times to fight for their love. My dad says they're all the same,
which . . . they are, but still, I'm a hopeless romantic.

I'm well aware that love stories, family relationships, and
friendships in real life are never like they are in the movies.

They aren't always rainbows and butterflies, made up of zero hard times. They're hard, messy, and confusing. They can be the biggest blessing, but they are also a ton of work.

With the heightened use of social media, we see posts and updates of who's in a relationship with who, who's getting married, who's having babies, who's hanging out together, and what friends are up to. If you aren't married, in a relationship, or having children by a certain age, then for some reason, you begin to convince yourself that you are "less than" those around you who seem to have it all figured out. Our lives seem less significant because we have yet to hit the "important" milestones our culture loves to celebrate.

When I was a kid, I thought by twenty-five I'd not only be married, but I'd have a baby of my own. It's funny how time works. It sure does fly, and it can turn out how we dreamed, or it can be a sharp contrast to what we had in mind.

How did my vision as a child look when I reached the ripe age of twenty-five? The opposite.

The year came and went, and I did not have even one of the things I had hoped for. As I sit and type this, I'm somehow already twenty-eight. At the time of publishing this, even more years have flown. I'm now thirty one and have a sweet little one we are so thankful to have.

My younger brother has been married to his high school sweetheart for four years, and they are the absolute most precious couple. They just had their first baby, who is so full of joy. Like any couple, they have their ups and downs, and I've seen them endure tough times. I know it's been a beautiful journey, but it hasn't been easy in every season. I have learned so much not only about romantic relationships, but friendships as well, by spending time around them.

Do you want to know the one thing that's characterized their relationship, that's been a key part of their strength and growth? They have always put Jesus first. In every single season. They sought Jesus, they turned to Him, and that's made all the difference. Christ has been at the center of their relationship from the start, and I've had the opportunity to watch that grow throughout the years. This created a desire within me to have a marriage that would also model Christ. I've always dreamed of a good, strong marriage, but I learned from them, a great marriage was built on Christ.

Seven years ago, I wrote a prayer in my journal to my future husband. I listed the qualities I desired in a husband and wrote about how excited I was to meet him. One of the key characteristics I noted was that He would love and pursue Jesus more than me. I didn't meet my future husband for the first time until four years later. A winding road of heartbreak occurred in that timeframe, but through it, I saw how good and gracious the Lord is.

Those four years, and the many before that, were years I spent praying for my future husband. At that time, I was navigating the "dating scene," which, might I say, was not one of my favorite scenes to walk . . . Throughout, I kept wondering when it would be my time.

One day, the sweet Lord led me straight through the doors of Anytime Fitness for a job opportunity, where I would meet and work beside my future husband. Was it love at first sight? Surprisingly, no! I had no idea, at the time I started there or for the first year of working there and building a friendship, that I would ever marry him, but guess who did?! GOD!! And guess what? It was His plan all along.

Compared to the guys I had dated in the past, getting to know my husband was not hard. It wasn't stressful to be in a relationship with him. I didn't feel like I had to be someone I wasn't. We laughed and joked and became best friends before dating even crossed my mind. Note: I did say my mind because DJ certainly had other plans.

I truly believe the strong foundation we developed as friends first makes our marriage so sweet. From the dates I had been on in previous years, I recognized one of the characteristics missing was friendship. Couples do not seem to understand where true friendship fits into their relationship. So often, we meet someone and put a label on it, almost overnight. There is no chance for the friendship stage because we are so excited to say we have a boyfriend or girlfriend before we take the time to truly get to know that person. I see it happen all of the time. I used to do the same thing. I dated someone just to date, sometimes doing so without any intention of ever marrying the person. In this day and age, doesn't it seem we'd rather label the "relationship" than learn about the person's heart? We'd rather speed it up than slow it down to learn who they are behind all of the walls that have been built over the years.

You are probably well aware we live in a generation of hook-ups, non-commitment, ghosting, and "talking." It's very rare for a man to even ask a woman to be his girlfriend anymore. I came across it all firsthand: men who cheated, lied, and one who didn't want to post pictures together, but wanted to hang out and "really liked me," yet wouldn't be ready to date for a while . . . The joys of dating. Instead of joy, though, we see a generation of confusion, heartbreak, leading people on, and damaging our future marriage before we even meet the person we're meant to marry.

What surprised me most about my relationship with my husband was how different it was from what's deemed "popular" in today's day and age. This sweet man was everything on the list I had created four years prior and even more. He pursued me, he asked me to be his girlfriend, and couldn't wait to do so. He held my hand in public, and was so proud and excited to call me his. Sometimes, I didn't know how to react because there were no doubts whatsoever in his mind. He never made me question or doubt where I stood with him. I never had to contemplate how to respond to his messages or calls, afraid of being *too much* for him, because I knew he was in it for the long haul. Even now that we're married, it's still hard sometimes because he's always so good to me, and it's far from what I was used to.

Revolutionizing Your Relationship Status

Unlike the examples I was given by society, where relationships and friendships can come and go and be replaced almost instantly, I witnessed and spent time with my brother and his wife, a healthy relationship that turned into a marriage. Commitment. Perseverance. Communication. They didn't give up when things got tough. They didn't push each other away when they were going through a tough season or when they got annoyed with one another. They didn't ignore each other when they had a disagreement or say hurtful things when they got upset. They never cheated and pursued other people on the side, even when faced with seasons of a long-distance relationship. They didn't lie about things. They remained faithful and committed to one another; they learned to communicate and work through things rather than avoid them and let them fester. They shared lessons they learned with me to help me become a better friend and eventual wife.

On one of our family vacations, before I was married, we took a boat out together and spent some time floating and swimming in the water. I picked their brains and asked about the challenges of marriage and what they had learned in the first two years. It's the wisdom they've shared throughout the different stages of their relationship that's helped me step confidently into marriage. It's the work I've done with my own heart and mindset that's prepared me to set up a successful, strong foundation with my husband. Is it perfect? Absolutely not. Even on the days we drive each other crazy, there is one thing that will forever be there at the root of our relationship. Our commitment we made to one another and the covenant of marriage. We will never run apart or peace out when times get tough. Through our marriage, you will see commitment over and over again.

In the book of Ruth, Ruth chooses to remain with her mother-in-law after her husband died. It would have been so easy for her to say sayonara, to continue and start a new life, somewhere else, with someone new. However, she had no intention to do that whatsoever. She refused to allow the separation to happen. Instead, she clung to her mother-in-law. She remained loyal when Naomi would have understood if she split.

> *At this they wept aloud again. Then Orpah kissed her mother-in-law goodbye, but Ruth clung to her. "Look," said Naomi, "your sister-in-law is going back to her people and her gods. Go back with her."But Ruth replied, "Don't urge me to leave you or to turn back from you. Where you go I will go, and where you stay I will stay. Your people will be my people and your God my God. Where you die I will die, and there I will be buried. May the Lord deal with me, be it ever so severely, if even death separates you and me."When Naomi realized that Ruth was determined to go with her, she stopped urging her.*
> Ruth 1:14-18, NIV

Is that how we react when things get hard or something significant happens in our friendships or relationships? Do we chalk it up as a loss and move on? Take a moment to reflect on those close relationships in your life with your family, friends, spouse, or colleagues. Are you in it for the long haul, portraying the loyalty Ruth showed Naomi? Or, do you often flee at the first argument, the first job offer at a different company, the first tension-filled emergency? Are you a Ruth, or are you a runner? Is it time you revolutionized your relationship status? Are you ready to become a better version of yourself that will impact personal and professional relationships?

Many don't want to put in extreme amounts of effort if it's required or wait for those special, long-lasting friendships or relationships. Others don't choose to seek love, guidance, and wisdom in healthy places. The media, commercials, movies, and everything around us can convince us that we should seek validation from others, that we should run at the first sight of tension or disagreement, or we must be in a relationship to be successful and to matter, so we settle. We become comfortable with the person or people in our lives who disrespect us and somehow believe we deserve that type of love, when we deserve so much more.

Revolutionizing Your Relationship Status

Sweet friend, your life has immense meaning and purpose, no matter your relationship status. If you're single: Break up with the thought that you have to be in a relationship to matter.

If you're in an unhealthy, toxic relationship: Break up with that person who's cheated on you more times than you can count or the one who physically or emotionally abuses you daily. You're worthy of so much more.

For those of you in a healthy friendship or relationship: Break up with the thought that you have to flee when times get tough. Perhaps that's how everyone in your family handled conflict and modeled relationships to you growing up, but be the one to divorce that pattern and break the generational curse. Be a Ruth in a world of runners.

I know you're thinking this is easy for me to say because I'm now married. But I was in your shoes. I've been put through the wringer of unhealthy and heartbreaking relationships. I longed to be married for years before I was. I sought Godly friendships that would better me. I cried tears of frustration and disappointment, and I tried to make things work that were not for me.

You see, when I tried to do it myself, it fell apart. When I handed it over to the Lord, He taught me I didn't have to be controlled by my relationship status. I was letting it control me, but He wanted control of my heart.

He wanted me to see and understand that I could enjoy life and that I still had a huge purpose, regardless of whether or not I had a significant other or the "right" friends in my life. The same is for you. You are not any less significant or any more important because of your relationship status.

Whatever season you are in right now—whether you're in a relationship, single, married, engaged, surrounded by friends or family, or lacking God-honoring relationships—find beauty in it. You are not defined by it. Remember who you are, not what you lack. You are a son or daughter of Christ, and you are loved, regardless of who you have in your life. Use this season to grow.

If you're single, use it for personal growth and development, for digging into the Word and becoming a more confident version of yourself.

If you're in a relationship, use it to grow together and determine if this person is the right one for you.

If you're married, use it to strengthen your marriage.

If you have a solid group of friends, become better together.

I've stayed in one too many relationships for one too many days because I was fearful. Fearful of being alone when everyone else had someone. Fearful of each day passing, getting a little bit older, and still no closer to the marriage I'd always prayed for. Fearful of being single forever. Fearful of being without someone. It sounds so dramatic when I look back, but I was so afraid and had such a strong desire to reach that stage in life that I let it overtake me.

After having my heart broken enough times, I finally laid it at Jesus' feet. I knew I couldn't control my future. But, I knew the One who was in control, the One who already knew if and when I would meet the man He created for me. So, rather than seeking a relationship with a man, I began seeking His heart and spending more time in His Word. I surrendered my timeline, future relationship, and marriage to Jesus. Surrendering to Him led me to the most precious realization: my singleness became a blessing.

For me, my season of singleness was one of the most beautiful times for me to grow in my relationship with the Lord. I knew that once I was married, I wouldn't have as much alone time for just Jesus and me. Someday, I will have a house full of a husband and a couple of kids. Life will be busy, and I won't be taking care of only myself.

Revolutionizing Your Relationship Status

There's beauty in singleness. I think we often rush past in order to get to the next season of dating and marriage, even if it isn't the right person. Some people will date just to say they're in a relationship and get married because they're lonely and don't want to wait. We sprint past seasons of being without many friends, just so we can have someone to hang out with, even if that means finding friends in unhealthy places that encourage you to sin just "for fun."

What could you do in the meantime though, rather than rushing into another destined to fail "relationship"? What can you do to prepare to be the best husband or wife to your future spouse? What can you do to become a better version of yourself, so you can impact and be a light to the family and friends around you? Rather than spending time wondering when you'll find your Mr. or Mrs. Right, what could you do now to become the best you that you can be? Are there insecurities or hurts you battle with each day? Do you need to work through those so you don't bring them into the future, hindering the growth of any friendships or relationships that come your way?

I love learning. I love the ideas about people gained from the Enneagram personality test and *The 5 Love Languages: The Secret to Love that Lasts* by Gary Chapman—anything that gives me a deeper understanding of why I do the things I do and where those things might stem from. Not only that, but these personality insights help me discover how I can better love and serve those around me, based on their love languages or Enneagram numbers. I hope it's a forever process for me—always seeking to improve myself. That's what my season of singleness was—learning from others, observing their relationships, reading books, asking questions, understanding the hurts I've experienced and how they've affected me, then learning to work through those disappointments so I don't carry unnecessary hurts from the past into my relationship and eventually into marriage. Have there still been things I have carried into marriage? Absolutely, but if I hadn't done any personal development before tying the knot, I know the baggage would have been heavier than the fifty-pound weight limit the airport gives us. In this case, though, I wouldn't be carrying it through the airport, I'd be carrying it into our marriage.

Look at whatever season you are in from the perspective of how you can make the most of it. Shift from believing it's a burden to declaring it a season of blessing. Do the things that bring you joy. Learn. Explore. Find your passions. Meet new people. Go on an adventure. Serve. Embrace every moment of those experiences.

No matter what challenges come, and they will, keep on keeping on. If you're going through a tough season with your spouse, remember, it won't last forever. What can you do to ease the tension between the two of you? What can you two do together that will help you to work through it, to make your relationship stronger? Think of your best memories. Focus on the things you love or value about your spouse. Remember why you married one another; what you loved about each other. To seek counseling or guidance from a professional does not make you weak; don't feel ashamed if you need to seek help. View it as a positive step to restoration. You know you need help, and you're seeking it. It will make you better in the long run.

If you're single or searching for healthy friendships, remember to fill your heart full of God's love for you. We all have a void in our hearts that we sometimes try to fill with other people. Another human being will never be able to satisfy that emptiness. Don't put that pressure on someone else, because it will never be satisfied by a person.

If you're unsure where to start, reach out to your church. See if they have any small groups for the age range you're seeking. Get connected. Being plugged into a church is so powerful. If you don't have a local church, do some research about what's in your area and visit. Get a feel for it. Look for local mom groups, young adult groups, or a group for your hobbies or passions. If nothing exists for what interests you, start a group! Create a simple flier, and post it around your community. Create an event on Facebook to invite people. There are people out there who enjoy similar things as you, just waiting for an opportunity to pursue them more!

Starting now, break free from the belief you must have a significant other or a certain group of friends to have significance in your life. There are great blessings in every season of life. You are special and so loved by God, and you don't need another person beside you to attain that love. With God, you will never be defined by your relationship status. You are loved recklessly, fiercely, forever and ever, right as you are, where you've been, and right where you're going. God is your Ruth, and He's clinging to you, every moment of every day.

Uncap the Pen:

Are you in a romantic relationship? Do you have a friend group? Are the relationships healthy? Have you ever stopped to think of what a healthy relationship means to you? List out the most important, nonnegotiable qualities you are looking for in your future spouse and friendships. If you're already married, list out the characteristics you desire in your marriage.

____

____

____

If you're currently dating someone, do they contain the qualities you listed above? If not, do you feel as if you're compromising what you desire in a spouse out of fear of being lonely or because you truly see a healthy future with this individual? Explain.

____

____

____

What did you learn through your season of singleness or waiting for a friend group? Do you feel the Lord did a work in you, or did you rush through it? Write a few sentences describing the most important things you learned or are currently learning.

____

____

____

Now, consider the future. What is something you always want to remind yourself of, no matter your age, no matter your relationship status? After you're married for forty years, or friends with people for fifty, when looking back in time to when you were younger, what do you always want to remember about this time and your prayers for marriage or friendships?

____

____

____

____

<u>Sign the Divorce Papers:</u>

"Lord, thank You for Your relentless love. Thank You for pursuing me, no matter the season, the day, or the time. Of all the things in this world, I know Your love is never ending and stronger than any emotion I face. When the burdens of life are heavy and my heart feels alone, You give me the strength to persist. I know You have the perfect plan for my life, and You will bring the people into my life that are meant to be a part of my story. Whether it looks like a friendship, a relationship or a marriage, I pray for the hearts of those I will encounter. I pray You use me as a light for them. I pray no matter what my relationship status is, that I come to truly know, understand, and be overwhelmed with how loved I am. I pray I honor You and keep a strong foundation built solely on You. I pray for openness and acceptance for whatever You have in store and pray I learn to trust and believe in Your perfect timing. Thank You for Your reckless love. I love You, Lord."

Marrying Freedom

Redefining Success

What does success mean to you?

Is it when you reach the "top" of the ladder, becoming the
CEO or the manager?
When you start your own business or work from home?
When your parents tell you they are proud of you?
When you make enough money to pay off your debts, and it
allows you the opportunity to travel as you please?

Maybe you feel successful already, and you have achieved
none of those things. Perhaps you will feel successful only
when you can check the box showing you accomplished one
of the goals above.

Over the past few years, I have found myself at many
networking events in communities across the state. It doesn't
matter where I am or what type of event it may be, upon
meeting someone new, the first question that comes out
after the introductions are made is, "So, what do you do?"

These days, we are no longer known by our name,
connected in some way to the person we're talking to by
parents, grandparents, or some other interesting ancestral
connection. Now it's commonplace to be known by our job
title or affiliated with the company or person we work for. It's
the first thing asked, and our response about what we do will
leave a first impression.

It often doesn't matter the type of person someone is at
heart or what someone does at their job. The title, company,
and connections have become what is important. When
someone asks what we do, the words spoken after that

pivotal question will leave the person feeling either extremely impressed or completely lackluster towards continuing a conversation. If we don't fit certain criteria or have rank or connections, we become just another face in the crowd. We see the conversation oh-so-conveniently interrupted when the person we're speaking to claims, "Excuse me while I have to take this phone call." An easy way out. And so, we become our job title.

It appears it doesn't matter if you volunteer three nights a week, you're on the prayer team at church, or a mentor for a less fortunate child; when you tell someone you work part-time as a cashier at a gas station, as an example, some people will automatically deem you as less than. It will deter them from future conversations.

Is a cashier any different than the CEO of a company? Perhaps the title, but guess what? Every human being was and is and always will be created by the same God of the universe as you and me. One might have more education, make more money, or have a more "important" job title than you, but each one of us is the same. It's time we learn to redefine success.

The Lord created us all equally, with such beautiful and intricate qualities that no one else in this world could ever possess. Each and every characteristic of your being was given to you for a very important reason. Everything about you He created with intention. Without you on this planet, there's a very important piece of this world, with a very special calling and purpose, that would be missing.

At the time I was writing this, I was driving and thinking, Man, I'm going to be twenty-seven this year. How in the world?! Then, I began thinking about where I was at in life and how different my journey has looked from those around me. It's been a wild ride full of contract jobs, travel, and writing when I can.

When people ask me what I do, I could let the fear of being

judged for where I'm at prevent me from being confident in how I respond, or I can boldly say where I'm at, what I'm doing, and where I plan to go from here. Telling others that my passion is to be a writer has been scary in the past. People's reactions to that pursuit can be quite negative. If I am not careful, their negativity can be internalized. The Devil will use those lies and negative thoughts to slowly creep into my mind during seasons of discouragement.

When I was a junior in college, one of my professors told me I would never make it in the marketing field. I was a literal wreck about the statement, but there was no way I was changing my degree, especially when I was only a year from graduation. Six years later, I'm doing well in my career, but I know, on days of deep frustration, those little lies of the enemy still try to squeeze their way in, even after all of these years . . . "You'll never make it. You're not good enough at what you do."

He will do the same to you. When you're discouraged, when you're going through a rough patch, he will bring those untrue, sarcastic remarks to the forefront of your mind. He'll keep doing that until you finally convince yourself that that person was right, you can't do it.

If you have goals and a plan in mind, I know from experience, you must be very careful with whom you share it. Other people's words have the potential and capability to help bring your dreams to life, but they can also stomp and shatter them on the ground, before they even start to bloom.

You have dreams you want to pursue that could lead to an opportunity for time and financial freedom. But you let the words of someone you confided in snap you back to "reality," you may never achieve those goals. That dream is too big; it's too crazy. So instead, you allow those words to take root and start to sow your seeds along the same route so many are on—the safe route. Instead of the freedom you knew was possible, you feel more and more trapped.

Marrying Freedom

People often find pride in working sixty hours a week, being busy, sleeping little, and feeling stressed. It's crazy to me when I hear people talking about being proud of it. It's become common for people who aren't consumed by their jobs to be given the stink eye, called lazy, or deemed weirdos. But, it's how our generation lives and people are afraid to stand out and be different. There's no end in sight. The cycle continues, and we fall deeper and deeper into overcommitting our hearts, minds, and souls to things that we, deep in our hearts, could care less about.

"I am so stressed out."
"I didn't even eat dinner last night, because I was working so late. Then, I went home and went straight to bed."
"I haven't seen my husband/wife all week because I've been at the office so much."

These are sentences we hear daily from those among us, almost as badges of honor. We listen and agree, and it seems as if it's acceptable. We slave away to our jobs, because we believe once we hit that next rung on the ladder, we'll have made it. Once we're promoted to manager, director, or partner, we'll slow down a bit to enjoy life. But for now, we'll dwindle to nothing but work—no free time, family time, or friend time, and no time to decompress and relax. Just the grind. "Rest is for the weak. I'll sleep when I'm dead."

We keep at that pace until the day comes when we realize we can't physically do it any longer.

Your health is taking a toll.
Your marriage is hanging on by a thread.
You don't sleep, barely eat, and consume an obnoxious amount of caffeine throughout the day, to make it through.
You haven't had an actual conversation with your children in weeks.
The list of negative consequences to this lifestyle goes on.

Yet, we find it so difficult to draw a line, even though it's demonstrated time and time again in the Bible. It's more than that, though—God created a day for us to rest. A day to take a step back. He made that day holy.

"The seventh day God had finished the work he had been doing; so on the seventh day he rested from all his work. Then God blessed the seventh day and made it holy, because on it he rested from all the work of creating that he had done."
Genesis 2:2-3, NIV

Did you catch that? He did the work, and then He took a break. He made a specific day for us to do the same. It's not a silly day or a day to skip over . . . No, it's holy. It's woven into Jesus' story. We see a pattern. Work, rest, repeat. It wasn't just a thing He tried every now and then. He made it a priority.

Taking the five loaves and the two fish and looking up to heaven, he gave thanks and broke the loaves. Then he gave them to the disciples, and the disciples gave them to the people. They all ate and were satisfied, and the disciples picked up twelve basketfuls of broken pieces that were left over. The number of those who ate was about five thousand men, besides women and children. Immediately Jesus made the disciples get into the boat and go on ahead of him to the other side, while he dismissed the crowd. After he had dismissed them, he went up on a mountainside by himself to pray. Later that night, he was there alone.
Matthew 14:19-23, NIV

He did the work He knew He needed to do, then He took time to fill His soul by going on his own to pray and be alone with the Lord. He knew it was vital. Yes, He was often around large groups of people, but that didn't prevent Him from retreating and recharging.

If the Maker of heaven and earth needed to take a break from doing, creating, serving, performing miracles, healing, and pouring into the lives of others, don't you think we'd be wise to do the same?

Don't you think it's necessary that we, too, learn where to draw that line?

Whether you have the job title of CEO, Manager, Executive, or Intern, it shouldn't matter. Regardless of what those at work call you, it is okay to take a break. Maybe you've never had someone tell you that. So, let me tell you again. Let me give you permission right now. It is completely okay to take a break. It is healthy to take a break. Jesus took breaks. Jesus had quiet times. Give yourself permission to do the same. You need it more than you're letting on.

Maybe it's been drilled into your heart, mind, and soul that taking a break, shutting your mind off, and taking time for yourself outside of work, are not okay. It's been ingrained by the people in your sphere that time off is unacceptable, cowardly, and unnecessary.

You believe only the "weak" take breaks, but because you've pushed yourself so long, you are now the weakest you've ever felt, emotionally, physically, spiritually, and mentally.

I'm not sure if you've noticed or not, but time doesn't stop for anyone. You might say "tomorrow" right now . . .

Tomorrow I will be better.
Tomorrow I will spend an hour with my family or friends.
Tomorrow I will be present when I'm at home and not have my laptop fired up with work-related tasks consuming my mind.
Tomorrow I will put down my phone when my spouse comes home from work and have an actual conversation.
Tomorrow I will put a limit on the number of hours I work.

Tomorrow, tomorrow, tomorrow . . . Tomorrow never comes.

Before you know it, we will be ten years, twenty-five years, down the road.

Redefining Success

Will you look back and be happy where you're at, or will you wish you'd have taken more time to fill your schedule with people and things that truly mattered to you, rather than filling it to the brim with appointments and physical items that had no special place in your heart?

I had this striking realization just a few months ago. I was running on fumes, mentally exhausted. I'd been wearing so many hats and trying to juggle so many things, and it was catching up to me. I'd been praying frequently about where I was headed, and I knew what I was doing was not what I was created to do. The longer I walked on that path, the clearer it became, and the more unrested, stressed, and unlike myself I became.

I won't lie to you: I strongly disliked myself at the time. Looking back, I'm quite ashamed of the way I let work take over my entire life. The to-do lists never ended, and I found myself barely speaking two words to my parents when I got home at the end of the night. Even if I did, it was often a few words before I opened up my laptop to get back to work. I was constantly thinking of work when I was away on a weekend trip. If one of my bosses called, it was as if I had to stop what I was doing on vacation and answer it.

One weekend, we were in our favorite town of Rolla, Missouri. The first time we visited, we were amazed by the beautiful countryside views. We learned quickly there was zero cell service amongst the rolling hills, which made it even more relaxing. It was a gorgeous, no cloud-in-the-sky Saturday. We were out hiking, exploring, swimming, and having the literal best time, not a care in the world. I didn't check my phone until early afternoon when we started driving back toward our hotel. When I did, I had a text from my boss asking for me to call him; it was important. I instantly tensed, became anxious, and couldn't stop checking to see if I had enough cell service to call him as we drove closer to the city limits.

It was as if a light switch had gone off, from carefree to combustible, in a matter of minutes. I had no boundaries for myself. I could have responded, "I will call on Monday morning," but instead, I dialed up as soon as I was able.

Every weekend, I found myself trying to catch up and maybe get a bit ahead on the coming weeks' work. It never happened. The lists only kept growing.

One Sunday afternoon, I finally couldn't handle it anymore. I knew I needed to change how I was living, but knew I needed to surrender it all to the Lord and trust He would provide me with the next step to take.

And guess what? He did just that. He led me away from that life and into His freedom, into a new understanding that I'm here on this earth for more than just a to-do list, for more than trying to wear five different hats and keep it all together. I was attempting to do everything for everyone who needed something, all while maintaining some sort of balance, which was never actually achieved. It was time to move on from that.

There will always be something that needs to be done. We live in an ever-changing world. You have to remember this: you are not your checklists. You are not the tasks. You are not the result of completing those items.

Whether you're at the top of the ladder, or you're just beginning, the title is irrelevant. Your education or salary, job title, or status in the community does not dictate your significance. Sure, you might think you're more important, better off, more deserving or entitled than the person next to you, but the truth is, you aren't.

Being at the top is no different than being at the bottom. The same God created us. We're all His sons and daughters. Your job title does not define you. If you think it does, then you're wrong. On this side of heaven, people might find great care and concern for their job title, but when we cross over into Heaven, it will hold no value whatsoever.

CEOs will not get into heaven easier than the garbage man.

Redefining Success

Owning five businesses will not give you higher priority in eternity than the individual who was fired. We're all the same. All who put their faith and hope in Christ will indeed end up in heaven, where we won't be competing and striving to hit the next rank. There will be no hierarchy. We'll be where we belong, and we won't have to put any effort into trying to make it in or fit in, because we'll be in our perfect and purest form.

Don't live a life convinced that where you work or what you're doing with your life defines who you are. You are so much more than a job title or success at work. You are a loved, chosen, and a valuable child of God. Remember the example we see modeled by Jesus. He did the work, but He didn't let it overrun His life. It's often in "the halt" that we can see, more clearly, where Jesus wants us to head. Oftentimes, we can accomplish more than we could in the hustle. The Lord is rest and offers rest to us.

Come to me, all you who are weary and burdened, and I will give you rest. Take my yoke upon you and learn from me, for I am gentle and humble in heart, and you will find rest for your souls.
Matthew 11:28-29, NIV

Your circle of people might be fully convinced that career success equals feeling entitled, special, and important.

However, we aren't to live to please and be so concerned with other people's opinions of us. Instead, we must remember that in God's eyes, success equals living a life that glorifies His kingdom and leads people to know Him. He wants us to realize how loved we are, no matter what "class" of society we are in.

God created you for a unique and specific purpose. Your calling and purpose might be completely different from what you were hoping for. It might seem crazy and ridiculous, or it might make total sense. You might hate where you are and what He's calling you to, but if He is in it, then there is an extremely important reason for it.

Maybe you feel disappointed because you think you deserve *more*. Maybe you're afraid because you feel He's calling you to something too big. No matter what it looks like, if He is in it, then I guarantee you, you need not be afraid. Remain faithful in the little things, just as much as you would the big ones. There is no position *unimportant*. Each and every step that He leads you on is with purpose. Only He knows why He has you where He has you; you just have to do your very best to live intentionally and as a "mini-Christ" to those you encounter.

There are people who have never picked up a Bible, who have never heard of the Bible or Jesus. For some, seeing the way you live your life may be the only example of Jesus they will ever see. Your life will be the only Bible they ever read.

When we look at our lives through those lenses, how does that impact the way we live and what we strive for?

Do you get upset and frustrated with your coworker when they interrupt your day to ask you a few questions, or do you show them patience, care, and appreciation for wanting to do a good job?
Do you yell at the barista for getting your order wrong, or do you tip them a little extra for taking the time to make your drink, even if they used almond milk instead of oat milk?
Do you take the time to show love and concern to your crying child, or do you brush them off and tell them to suck it up because you have to hit a deadline?

If we claim to be Christians, then shouldn't we be showing the fruits of the Spirit to everyone we encounter? Remember this verse: "But the fruit of the Spirit is love, joy, peace, forbearance, kindness, goodness, faithfulness, gentleness, and self-control" (Galatians 5:22-23, NIV). Shouldn't we be showing these qualities and this love and concern in our daily lives?

You are no better off or less than anyone you encounter.

To the world, it might be about titles, certificates, and promotions, but to Christ, it's about us, as we are. It's about putting His Kingdom, His glory, and His purpose into motion right where we are, with exactly what we have, with the people right by our sides.

You don't have to compete for or achieve His love. It's freely given. To me, being a child of God is by far the best title to ever receive. Is it yours?

Uncap the Pen:

Do you believe with your whole heart that those around you are all created equal? What can you do today that will show those you interact with that we are each created equally, regardless of titles?

____

____

____

Take a look at your daily life. Are you proud of the way you are living? Do you feel as if you're living for more than just your daily lists? Are you being present with the people around you?

____

____

____

In what ways can you be more like Christ right where you are? Are there certain tasks, jobs, or conversations you have daily that you should carry out in a different manner?

____

____

____

Next time you meet someone, what are some other questions you can ask to get to know them better? Can you have a conversation without asking their job title? How do you think this will feel?

____

____

____

<u>Sign the Divorce Papers:</u>

"Dear God, I want to thank You. Thank You for being my strength. Thank You for opening my eyes to see as You see, for the realization we are all created equally and with significant purpose, a purpose that is not always tied to our work successes. Thank You for aligning me with the people and opportunities that are necessary to complete that purpose. Thank You for helping me close the doors that need shut, and for giving me the strength to open the doors that might look a little scary. Give me the courage to be the person you want me to be. God, I believe with my entire heart I was put in this world for more than just a job. Help me to shine brightly for You to the people I interact with on a daily basis. Thank You for Your relentless pursuit of my heart. You are more than words can say, and I'm grateful for the way You love me enough to show me grace and mercy. Give me eyes to see, and grant me a heart to feel as You do. Help me show that to those I encounter in every instance."

Persevering After Abandonment

*Consider it pure joy, my brothers and sisters, whenever
you face trials of many kinds, because you know that
the testing of your faith produces perseverance. Let
perseverance finish its work so that you may be mature
and complete, not lacking anything.*
James 1:2-4, NIV

Has anyone ever walked out of your life? Just up and left?
There one day, a distant memory the next? It's weird to think
how someone can be a big part of your life for any amount
of time, then one day, they're just not there anymore.

They might have moved hundreds of miles away, never to
be seen again. Perhaps someone slipped out of sight just like
a ghost. They aren't far away in distance, yet you have no
clue where they are because you no longer communicate
with one another. Maybe it's not a "they moved away and
abandoned me" situation. It could be you still pass that
person in the car and run into them at the grocery store,
but that person wants nothing to do with you. For some, it's,
"I know we're family, and even though you didn't do anything
to hurt me, I still can't stand to look at you."

The current situation might or might not be your choice.
Either way, whether you will admit it or not, it is likely to have
an impact on you in some way. Without realizing it, the roots
may have been sown, and there deep down, hidden in the
depths of your heart, lies the betrayal, guilt, and rejection
you felt from this desertion.

We ask ourselves, what did I do that caused them to leave?
Or maybe, why have they never wanted to be a part of my
life? What could I have done differently to make them stay?
What could I have done to make them want to be involved
in the big and small memories of my life? Maybe it was
absolutely beyond your control, yet the question still lingers.

Marrying Freedom

We want to put the blame on ourselves. We think, day after day, about what we said, what we did, or what we failed to do that could have impacted their decision and convinced them to stay. For some, it goes all the way back to birth and being put up for adoption, or having one parent leave while we were young. Again, we're not to blame, but we often try to put the blame on ourselves just to make sense of it all. We crave the answers, the reasoning. We cry out, "Answer me quickly, Lord; my spirit fails. Do not hide your face from me or I will be like those who go down to the pit" (Psalm 143:7, NIV).

We want His answers, or else we feel we will spiral into a pit of anguish and hurt that buries us.

Abandonment can be experienced in families, relationships, and friendships. It doesn't matter the setting or situation, the pain that results from it is often never anticipated or wanted. How can we persevere after someone abandons us?

I remember two occasions where I experienced the utter sting of abandonment, both of which happened within a few weeks of each other. One, with a gentleman I had grown very fond of; the other from a family member living next door. They held different levels of care in my heart, and I can still picture vividly the look in their eyes in those moments.

I'd walked next door to visit, not knowing it'd be the last time I'd ever see her in her home. It'd be the final time I'd see her in person and alert, while she was still on this side of heaven. As I left, she made it clear I'd done something wrong, though I had no idea what. From the look in her eyes, you could tell she wanted nothing to do with me.

Not long after, I stopped to say "hi" to a friend, as I'd done many times before, but something about this time felt different. It felt final, even if we didn't express it face-to-face. The conversation felt forced rather than easy and open like in previous weeks. The look in his eyes was distant. I didn't want to acknowledge it, so I played it off, trying to make light of the conversation. As I hugged him goodbye, something told me that would be it. Turns out, it would be the last time I'd see him until four years later, as we saw each other in passing. No explanation. Even after being so close for the previous few months, there was no closure, just a simple four-word text that said this was it. It was like a ghost slipping out of view.

Two people, who wanted nothing more to do with me. It didn't matter how badly I wanted to embrace them and talk through what was happening, to be adults, having a conversation about what each was experiencing.

Instead of embracing one another, we embarked on becoming distant memories in each other's lives. It's a different kind of hurt when you can't control anything, and for me, it meant long days and nights that didn't seem to get easier as months passed. The tears I cried probably could have filled a few water bottles. Dreams woke me from my sleep and kept me up half the night. I had zero desire to eat much of anything. It was an unhealthy season, physically and mentally. You wouldn't know by talking to me that I was immersed in the inadequacy I felt. I was the queen of hiding it from anyone and everyone. I had a smile glued to my face, and to everyone around me, I was radiating optimism galore. Deep down, in my own space, though, it was a different story.

This season was, hands down, one of the most challenging, but it's also where I leaned into God more than I ever had. The prayers and crying out to God when I couldn't understand what was happening ignited my faith in a way I hadn't experienced. Internally, my soul felt as if I had burned to ashes, and with that, I knew God promised, "To all who mourn in Israel, he will give a crown of beauty for ashes, a joyous blessing instead of mourning, festive praise instead of despair" (Isaiah 61:3, NLT). That's just what He did.

With time and digging into the Word of God, the pain became a little more bearable and less painful. Tears flowed less. The knots in my stomach became something I was accustomed to and barely noticed. I threw myself into my career and kept chugging along, which wasn't the best idea, either.

Avoiding my feelings and running away from what was going on, or in my case, throwing myself into anything and everything other than working through my pains, only led to more pain, empty feelings, and obligations that left me unfulfilled. Yes, I was praying through the season, but I wasn't pressing into God and allowing Him to have my complete heart in it. I was trying to do work on my own that could "fix" me, but really all I needed was to let Him repair all of the damage done.

In the simple, day-to-day moments, as occurred with Moses while he was tending sheep, the Lord showed me and helped me understand. Yes, it may have felt like I was a bush that was physically burning, but He was removing the wrong people to make room for the relationships representative of Him. He taught me that some people are only meant to be in our life for a season and not a lifetime.

Have you ever contemplated that maybe abandonment is setting you up for abundance?

In Exodus 1, we read of Pharaoh and his growing concern about the increase in the Hebrew population. He ordered: "Every Hebrew boy that is born you must throw into the Nile, but let every girl live" (Exodus 1:22, NIV). However, not every newborn male was killed, as Pharaoh hoped and planned.

Now a man of the tribe of Levi married a Levite woman, and she became pregnant and gave birth to a son. When she saw that he was a fine child, she hid him for three months. But when she could hide him no longer, she got a papyrus basket for him and coated it with tar and pitch. Then she placed the child in it and put it among the reeds along the bank of the Nile. His sister stood at a distance to see what would happen to him.

Then Pharaoh's daughter went down to the Nile to bathe, and her attendants were walking along the riverbank. She

*saw the basket among the reeds and sent her female slave
to get it. She opened it and saw the baby. He was crying,
and she felt sorry for him. "This is one of the Hebrew
babies," she said.*

*Then his sister asked Pharaoh's daughter, "Shall I go and
get one of the Hebrew women to nurse the baby for you?"
"Yes, go," she answered. So the girl went and got the
baby's mother. Pharaoh's daughter said to her, "Take this
baby and nurse him for me, and I will pay you." So the
woman took the baby and nursed him. When the child
grew older, she took him to Pharaoh's daughter and he
became her son. She named him Moses, saying, "I drew
him out of the water."*
Exodus 2:1-8, NIV

Moses grew, and one day, he saw an Egyptian beating a
Hebrew, one of his own. He killed the Egyptian and hid him
in the sand (Exodus 2:12, NIV). Word got around to Pharaoh,
so he attempted to kill him. Moses escaped, traveling to live
in Midian.

But then, the story takes a turn in the most ordinary of
moments—when Moses was tending the flock of his father-
in-law. He saw a bush that was on fire but wasn't burning
up, so he went to check it out. The Lord spoke to Moses
through it.

*The Lord said, "I have indeed seen the misery of my people
in Egypt. I have heard them crying out because of their
slave drivers, and I am concerned about their suffering. So
I have come down to rescue them from the hand of the
Egyptians and to bring them up out of that land into a good
and spacious land, a land flowing with milk and honey—the
home of the Canaanites, Hittites, Amorites, Perizzites, Hivites
and Jebusites. And now the cry of the Israelites has reached
me, and I have seen the way the Egyptians are oppressing
them. So now, go. I am sending you to Pharaoh to bring my
people the Israelites out of Egypt."*
Exodus 3:7-10, NIV

Marrying Freedom

While tending the flock, his moment had arrived. He was going to be used to lead others out of their oppression and suffering and into a life of abundance. He didn't rise from abandonment to appointment overnight. He wasn't affectionately accepted. No, he even had to ditch where he grew up and flee from the wrath of Pharaoh.

We have that same opportunity. However, deliverance will look different for everyone. Abundance, to you, will look, sound, and be different than it will for me. For some, it will be a happy ending with restoration or rekindlement. For others, it won't, but the Lord has other plans that will bring a different type of fortune into their lives. If I'm honest with you, my story didn't end with restoration. I won't lie to you and tell you I pushed through those weeks, and now it doesn't bother me at all. I attempted to make amends on the phone but was left with unanswered, unreturned calls. There were days I wanted to go to their houses and make everything okay. There are nights I would wake from dreams about them and get so angry at the way things are, how it all played out. In the moments when I see them from afar, sometimes those feelings of pain, emptiness, and sorrow all start to stir again. There are still moments when I let those thoughts into my mind, questioning why they made the decisions they did and whether it is, in some way, my fault?

But then, I remember the gentle reminder from our Savior; some people are meant to be in our lives only for a season. People will come and go, and sometimes, there's absolutely nothing we can do about it. That doesn't mean our lives must be any less beautiful because of someone's absence.

How, then, do we continue living when someone who played a big part in our life leaves? How do we continue not knowing what a relationship with a parent could have been if we have never met them? How do we keep persisting and living a happy life of freedom when we feel so weighed down by the thoughts of what went wrong, what could have been, and what should be?

Persevering After Abandonment

Well, when I was crawling through that season—and yes, I say crawling, because most of the time, I was on my knees praying to Jesus, because that's all I could do—I slowly learned a different side of who Jesus is. I knew He loved me. I knew that He promised, "As I was with Moses, so I will be with you; I will never leave you nor forsake you" (Joshua 1:5, NIV). I knew His faithfulness in so many things, but I was learning to find comfort in a whole new area of His steadfastness.

He'd been there before. He'd been through every trial, every tear, and He wasn't about to leave me now. He never left Moses. He saw him through as he lay in his basket in the Nile, and remained with him as he delivered the people from their oppression. He was always there. His presence is with you, as well. He isn't leaving you. Sure, it might seem silly to find fulfillment and comfort from someone you can't physically see or spend time with, but He is there.

Some of us think moving on might come through acceptance, forgiveness, and understanding. However, that won't always be the case. What our hearts need is Jesus. We won't understand everything that happens while we're here on the earth, but He understands every bit of how we feel. He can be anything and everything we need Him to be. Peace, joy, comfort, healing, mending, and fulfillment.

Day by day, I found more peace through seeking Him, reading His word, and coming to understand who He is on a deeper level. I became very independent over those couple of years. It was me and Jesus, and that's all I needed.

The opinions, the actions, and the coming and going of people in my life affected me less and less because where I found my fulfillment wasn't from other people. Humans can be fragile, even flaky, and sometimes fleeting; that's just the cold hard truth. Their feelings can change based on circumstances or how their day is going—on the smallest of things.

Jesus is unchanging. He is a firm foundation, a solid rock upon which we can build our lives. He's the one constant we can always depend on. No, trusting Him and living for Him doesn't mean no one will ever abandon you, no one will ever hurt or reject you, or no one will cause you pain and feelings you don't want to feel. It doesn't mean life will be easy.

It will be tough. There will be challenges. People will unexplainably leave. Look for His blessings in those moments you don't understand, even if you have to squint your eyes. Can you see the good that comes out of it? Those people that left, be it your mother, father, grandparent, sibling, friend, boyfriend, girlfriend, fiancé, husband, or wife . . . Those people don't determine your value or your worth.

Don't let them hold you captive. Don't hold on to the bitterness, the hate, and the regret. The enemy wants you with every ounce of his being. He wants you to hold a grudge against them forever and a lifetime, and to never forgive them. He wants you to recall that pain every single day, so you dwell in it and never give it up. A part of you wants to hold on to the pain, because it makes you feel as if you have some control or power over the situation.

Friend, that is not the type of fulfillment you want or need in your life. You do not want that bitterness and anger to be the crutch you lean on to walk through your days. You will walk taller and stand straighter with the Lord and His strength. Don't cower at the lies of the Devil, but instead, cruise into prayer.

Pray about it. Use prayer as your weapon. If you see that person who hurt you, pray for them. If you drive past their house, shower their home with prayers. If someone you know is talking about them and it stirs up those feelings, pray about it. If you never see that person and are hurt by that, lean into prayer.

It might not be easy; it might be the hardest thing you ever do, and it might make zero sense at all to pray for them and forgive them, especially when they've hurt you so badly in ways that you haven't talked about to anyone. Allowing that person to have control over you, to always have that in the back of your mind, will never do you any good.

At some point, the opportunity might arise, and you might come across them. You may have the urge to use words as a dagger to their heart, to express what you've bottled up, but what good will that do?

I know it's all messed up and unfair and might be one of the most painful things you've ever felt, and I'm so sorry you have to feel those emotions and go through this. I'm sorry he, she, or they left you. I'm sorry for how that makes you feel every single day. I'm sorry if that is something that stings and will stick with you every single day for the rest of your life. I'm sorry if you never received or will never receive an explanation as to why.

Nothing I say can take that pain away or make it any better. Just take heart. Lean into Jesus. Find a way to express what you're feeling—try journaling it, speaking with a professional, or talking with a trusted friend. Find hope and trust in knowing that what the Lord takes away, He has a purpose, and will replace it with something better. You will still lead a full life. Think of Moses. He was abandoned as a baby and would later lead the people of God out of oppression. Maybe you don't see it and maybe you don't understand how it could ever be any better. I can't promise you it will, but I can promise you Jesus knows your heart, He knows exactly what you need, and He will fill that void.

Take a look around you. What people are in your life? Has He led you to friendships, conversations, or opportunities that have blessed you in some way? Through the pain, have you noticed an unveiling of abundance in some area of your life?

Those people that walked out of my life left voids in my heart that I desperately sought to fill for years. But, there's such beauty in what the Lord has done in my heart through these situations and what he has taught me through it.

He's brought beauty from the ashes, and He can and will

use any fire that brings destruction to your life to create something beautiful. The fire may leave you with nothing but dust after He extinguishes the flames. Where the ash and dust lay is the perfect foundation to rebuild. Dust that He can form and mold and build into something wonderful—a treasure, a gem. He has your life in the palm of His hands, and He won't leave you smoldering.

Uncap the Pen:

Has there been a person, or people, in your life that have abandoned you? List him/her/them below.

____

____

____

Do you block out thoughts of this person or these people? Let's walk through those waters right now, and bring them to mind. What emotions do you feel when you think of this person/these people? If there is more than one person, you might feel differently about each individual. List out the sentiments you feel for each individual on your list.

____

____

____

____

____

Persevering After Abandonment

This will be the tricky part. Rather than harboring negative emotions for each instance listed above, see through Jesus' eyes of forgiveness. Write a short prayer for these individuals. Yes; it might seem silly or challenging to pray for these people, but trust the Lord to work through this with you. He will give you strength. Only He can give you the power to release this chain. We're called to forgive as God has forgiven us.

____

____

____

____

____

How do you feel after this contemplation and praying for those who have hurt you through abandonment? Do you feel any different?

____

____

____

____

Forgiveness and acceptance won't happen overnight. Don't think that by praying one prayer, everything will be fine and dandy. It's been years for me praying these types of prayers, and I still struggle. Begin praying for these people and for your own heart every day. See what changes you begin to notice in your life. Come back to this page in a month, and write down what you've noticed.

____

____

____

____

____

____

Sign the Divorce Papers:

"God, I know things will happen that I will never understand on this side of heaven. I might not ever be given a reason why this person walked out or why they chose not to be a part of my life. Give me the strength to walk through the abandonment with You. Give me a soft heart full of forgiveness, even when I am not given an apology, an explanation, or restoration. Fill my mind with the thoughts You think towards me, of the fulfillment I experience in You. I know I am fearfully and wonderfully made, that I am loved unconditionally by You, and that You will never leave me or forsake me. Let Your promises be all I need to fill my heart to the brim, overflowing with Your love. You created me, You know the deepest desires of my heart, and I trust You with this pain. Be my healer, mender, comfort, and peace through these trials. Thank You for giving me eyes to see as You do, a heart to love as You love. You are all I need, Lord."

Putting a Stop to People-Pleasing

God tested us thoroughly to make sure we were qualified to be trusted with this Message. Be assured that when we speak to you we're not after crowd approval—only God approval. Since we've been put through that battery of tests, you're guaranteed that both we and the Message are free of error, mixed motives, or hidden agendas. We never used words to butter you up. No one knows that better than you. And God knows we never used words as a smoke screen to take advantage of you.
1 Thessalonians 2:4-5, MSG

Raise your hand if you over-commit. That is, if you have any free hands to raise because you are so tied up in commitments, activities, and tasks, you can't put anything down to lift said hand.

We are all guilty of saying "yes" when we shouldn't have, at one time or another. Why do we do this to ourselves? We know what our schedules look like and how much we can handle without going bonkers, yet we commit past the point of being able to fulfill our obligations with the intentions and attitudes that it deserves.

Sure, your schedule is full, but . . .

Your neighbor is going out of town and needs a cat sitter. You hate cats, but you'd feel awful saying no, since you'll be around and don't have a ton of things going on. You say, "Sure, bring him over." That simple agreement cues four days of unnecessary stress. Not to mention, the cat doesn't do well with unfamiliar settings, so he keeps you up meowing all night and claws a hole in your sofa.

You have a full to-do list of items that needed to be done at work last week, yet it's still not done. Your coworker needs a little assistance on a project and comes to you for help.

Marrying Freedom

You know it'll increase your stress if you help, decreasing the quality of your work, but as long as you're helping a brother or sister out, your boss will understand, right?

Or have you been in this situation? You have a big weekend ahead of you—an important presentation on Saturday morning for your job that could lead to a promotion. However, it's your friend's birthday, so you feel obligated to go out. You're convinced your friend will never forgive you if you miss it, so you drag yourself out. You show up, mingle, play some games, stay up way too late, and feel groggy the next day. Turns out, there were so many people there, your friend had the chance to say hello and that was it. She wouldn't have been upset at all if you'd chosen to stay home and take care of yourself.

Maybe you're someone who feels like you're running on a hamster wheel at your job. Your day-to-day responsibilities aren't terrible by any means, but it's not where your passion lies. You feel caught in a continual cycle, and you're not sure how you're ever going to get out. The last thing you want is to let your coworkers, or even worse, your boss down. You're afraid of what others would think or say if you took the leap and pursued the path God has laid on your heart. Instead of putting in your notice, you stay paralyzed in that role, for the next fifteen years.

I'm sure you can describe a situation similar to those above that you've experienced in your own life. A time when you've put yourself in or stayed in a situation because you were afraid of letting someone down.

You don't want to let others down, but all the while, you're letting yourself down. You let things continue to pile onto your plate until you're sleeping three hours a night and consuming more cups of coffee in a day than you can count.

Which side of the coin are you on? "Am I now trying to win the approval of human beings or God? Or am I trying to please people? If I were still trying to please people, I would not be a servant of Christ" (Galatians 1:10, NIV). Are you living to please people, or practicing seeking the Lord and what He wants for you? Perhaps it's a toss-up, depending on the day?

Are you going through the motions of your days to create a certain image for those in your circle, or are you doing it because you know it's what God is calling you to?

The thing is, our days aren't and shouldn't, by any means, be an all-you-can-eat buffet, like a plate that's filled to the brim. Plates weren't created for you to pile steak upon potato upon dessert, all on one, just as our days aren't meant for stacking up responsibility upon extracurriculars upon work or school functions. However, here you are . . . Your plate is full and overflowing, and some items on the plate are hanging off the side by a thread. You're grumpy at best, and your mind never stops spinning, thinking of your endless to-do list. You're anxious and high-strung, and you don't even recognize yourself.

It's ironic . . . Have you ever noticed our generation, millennials, struggle with commitment? We won't get into a committed relationship because someone "better" might come along. We don't want to put down any roots and commit to one career for an extended period of time, because an opportunity with better pay and benefits might come along. We can't plan get-togethers, dates, or weekend plans in advance because we want to see what is going on that day or evening before committing to anything, because FOMO (fear of missing out).

We lack commitment, yet we don't bat an eye at over-committing time and resources to things that often leave us feeling unfulfilled and drained. We say yes after yes until there is zero time left for chance, for opportunity to strike, for time to just go with the flow and see what the Lord does in those moments. Days go from being fully lived to living full—full of penciled-in appointments that take us away from the things that we deep-down want to do.

Marrying Freedom

Say you're super passionate about writing, drawing, singing, or creating. If you could do that every day, and make enough money to get by, you would, hands down! However, you're afraid to take the risk and try it out, because there are no certainties that it would pay off. God's been nudging you to take that step with Him, but you're afraid. So, you sit in a cubicle for fifty-five hours a week doing a job that you are bored with and have no passion for, but it pays awesome, has benefits, and allows you to save a ton of money.

You had every intention of working on improving and pursuing your passions on the side until you could quit your day job and pursue your dream full-time, but by the time you get home at night, it's time to eat and go to bed, so you can wake up by 5 a.m. and do it all over again the next day. You've realized your job is full of trivial tasks that zap your energy, leaving you with no creative capacity and zero desire to do anything but sleep once you're finally home.

A few months ago, God laid on my heart that what I was doing wasn't where He wanted me long-term, and He was going to call me out of my comfort zone. He made it clear on multiple occasions, and I was terrified at what that meant. I'd have to have conversations with the people I care most about regarding what God might be calling me to do. I was comfortable where I was. I was happy. Sure, I was working crazy hours, but it didn't feel like work because I enjoyed it. I loved my coworkers more than anything. I loved the people I saw every day.

Okay, God . . . Why, when I get comfortable and into a role I enjoy, are you going to tell me that this isn't where you want me? His response: "It is better to take refuge in the Lord than to trust in humans" (Psalm 118:8, NIV). I had begun to trust myself and the plans I made for my days more than I was trusting the Lord, and He was calling me back to Him. The schedule I was creating was not *His*, but mine. I was doing more and more, but drifting further and further from Him. The busier I became, the less time I spent with Him, and the more I depended on my strength and discretion to make decisions. Not an ideal situation.

During my two-hour commute, He laid it on my heart that He was going to do some rearranging in my life. I might not have known what was next, but I knew the One who did, and that meant I was going to step into uncertain waters and trust He would provide. I felt convicted over and over again that I was not living the way God intended.

After much prayer and multiple conversations with my boss, as well as a possible opportunity for a new career path, we devised a plan. We determined an end date for my current role and what the transition would look like. I'd assist with training the staff that would take over my responsibilities, and then I'd launch into my new role. Here I was, putting in my notice, when I wasn't even guaranteed this other position. Great idea, right?

Well, it was. Sure people might think I'm insane, and yes, I was scared of not having another position at the end of that month. Yet, I felt complete peace about it and knew the Lord would direct me—I just needed to trust in Him.

Many of my conversations during that season started with, "You might think I'm crazy, but God . . . "

But God has put it on my heart that I'm not supposed to stay here.
But God has shown me He's going to use me in different ways than this.
But God brought these people to speak this into my life, on separate occasions, without the others knowing they, too, were telling me the same thing.

I'm sure some people were thinking, *This girl has lost it,* when I had those conversations. That's fine with me, though.

When I started to consider what others would think of my decision, I had to stop and remind myself who I was and would continue to live for. Would I be more concerned with pleasing God or pleasing other people?

It's a tough one. We want to please God, but we don't want to let our parents, friends, or coworkers down. We see them daily, we have to answer their questions and hear their thoughts on our paths, even if it's unwarranted advice. They're concerned about our here and now, but God is thinking of our eternity, and not solely ours, but those lives we come into contact with regularly as well. Their eternities are also at stake.

I was having a conversation about my dreams one day, and my good friend said, "Right now, you're living to not disappoint other people, but you're disappointing yourself." Talk about a dagger to the heart!

He knew I wanted to write. He knew I was the most passionate about it, but I was letting all other tasks and responsibilities take priority over what I was passionate about. Why? Because as long as I was hustling and grinding with work, then I would appear to other people that I'm "doing something with my life." If I were to stay at home and write, people would deem me lazy.

Can you relate to that? You enjoy where you're at, or maybe you don't, but you're not pursuing what you're passionate about because of what other people might think.

I knew I needed to draw a line, and after that conversation, I felt a shift in where I was going. I was going to write the book; I was going to prioritize time each day to write. I was going to do it. And guess what? You, holding this book, means I did.

It felt like such a weight lifted to pursue what I loved. No, it wasn't easy, and yes, I had to learn and continue to learn, day by day, how to prioritize my time. It meant saying no to things. It meant waking up early or squeezing in time between the demands of the day. It meant taking time, at the end of the day, to write instead of watching TV or doing something else. It meant spending an entire Saturday with my headphones in and my fingers typing away.

It meant saying no to people to say yes to God.

We can see a prime example of this in the story of Daniel when he was selected for training to enter the king's service. He was supposed to follow a certain diet but knew there were menu items that were considered impure under the law. He had a choice to make: to please the king or remain obedient to God.

Daniel resolved not to defile himself with the royal food and wine, and he asked the chief official for permission not to defile himself this way. Now God had caused the official to show favor and compassion to Daniel, but the official told Daniel, "I am afraid of my lord the king, who has assigned your food and drink. Why should he see you looking worse than the other young men your age? The king would then have my head because of you."

Daniel then said to the guard whom the chief official had appointed over Daniel, Hananiah, Mishael, and Azariah, "Please test your servants for ten days: Give us nothing but vegetables to eat and water to drink. Then compare our appearance with that of the young men who eat the royal food, and treat your servants in accordance with what you see." So he agreed to this and tested them for ten days.

At the end of the ten days they looked healthier and better nourished than any of the young men who ate the royal food. So the guard took away their choice food and the wine they were to drink and gave them vegetables instead.

To these four young men God gave knowledge and understanding of all kinds of literature and learning. And Daniel could understand visions and dreams of all kinds.

At the end of the time set by the king to bring them into his service, the chief official presented them to Nebuchadnezzar. The king talked with them, and he found

none equal to Daniel, Hananiah, Mishael and Azariah; so they entered the king's service. In every matter of wisdom and understanding about which the king questioned them, he found them ten times better than all the magicians and enchanters in his whole kingdom.
Daniel 1:8-20, NIV

It will not mean zero challenges in life when you decide to pursue what God is calling you to. It might mean saying no to what everyone else is saying yes to, as Daniel did with the royal food and wine. I think sometimes people fall into the trap of believing that, because they're saying yes to God, means that the rewards will come without effort; things will fall into place without setbacks, and the results will come overnight, not once encountering a hiccup. I hate to break the news to you, but this is not the case, my friend. I can almost promise you it will be challenging; it will take dedication, prayer, belief in yourself, and recommitting to your dreams, day after day.

Something else it will require? Accountability. The Lord created us to be in relationship with others; it's something we all need. However, you must be very careful of who your accountability partners are. The feedback those people give you will impact your determination and belief. The words that flow into your ears from your circle of people will either build you up or they'll tear you down, before you've taken the first step. If you tell the wrong people what's on your heart while your dream is still in seed form, it could be detrimental. Their words could suffocate the seed before it even has a chance to take root.

If they tell you it won't happen, it's a dumb idea, and it'll never work, aren't you going to believe them?

If they tell you you should prioritize work and not take any time off, because you need the money, will that guilt you away from chasing your dream?

Find the people that will support and encourage you, that will pray for you and speak life into your passions.

Putting a Stop to People-Pleasing

My husband and I were sitting on a merry-go-round at a park during a date in our early relationship days. We were having a "life chat", and he got this serious look on his face. I was nervous to ask what he was thinking about. He'd just asked me a few minutes before if I believed I could write a book and if I felt that was what God wanted me to do.

My response was, "Absolutely, yes." I was 110% certain of it, and I shared with him the different occurrences that led to this assurance.

There was silence for a little bit, as we both sat in our thoughts. He broke the silence, "Okay, here's what you're going to do . . . "

Oh boy. What's he going to say?

"On Monday, Friday, Saturday, and Sunday, you're going to send me pictures to show you spent an hour writing that day. I'm going to set a reminder on my phone, so I will make sure to ask you to send them to me."

I don't know about you, but I've never had someone believe in me or my dreams as much as he, and it brought tears to my eyes. He wasn't going to let me not write it. Find cheerleaders like that!

I knew I had been living to please other people, but it was time to stop. It was time to prioritize what I knew God had been calling me to for far too long. Now I was ready to develop and pursue the gifts the Lord has blessed me with. If He was going to use me in this world as a writer to share parts of my testimony, I was going to do it. If He wanted me to be vulnerable, regardless of how nervous it made me, I'd muster up the courage to do it.

He'd brought me through so much. He'd strengthened me, molded me, prepared me for this, and now, it was time to stop living for others. I would persist like Daniel and knew that, like him, the Lord would fill me with the wisdom and understanding I needed to fulfill the plans he had for me. My focus shifted from winning others to winning souls for Jesus—to bring His love and kindness to those around me.

I was ready to share His faithfulness, to inspire, to teach readers who Jesus is, and to help them discover a new level of freedom in their lives.The world is getting crazier by the day, and it needs more love and hope. There are people out there who need to know who Jesus is, and I needed and wanted nothing more than to commit my life to writing and sharing with believers and unbelievers alike.

Maybe you're reading this, and you don't know Jesus. Maybe you've known Him your entire life. Whichever you fall under, remember this: Whether you believe it or not, God does have the perfect plan for you—one that might not please every single person you encounter, but one that is unique and special just for you. There is no one else that can do it better. Not a single person on this planet can carry out what He created you for. Only you can do it, as He intended. He needs you to be all He created you to be.

Perhaps you're uncertain how to begin, wondering how I started and what's helped me overcome living a life trying to please others and gain their approval, affection, and affirmation.

The truth is, it's Jesus. His Word. Prayers for discernment, wisdom, guidance, and courage. Prayers that He opens and closes doors to show me where He wants me. Taking time to just sit and be with Him, to give Him a space where He can drop things on my heart and mind, then praying that I allow His voice to be louder than the voice of approval from others, than the distractions and lies of this world. I surround myself with other fellow believers who I can turn to for prayer, advice, and encouragement. I soak up every bit of love, truth, and fellowship I can. Start small. Come up with an action plan; then, don't let anything or anyone hold you back.

My heart and soul know He is always the answer. If I'm not living to please Him, if I'm not committing my time to things that He is in, that He is nudging me towards, then what am I living for? The things of this world, and those things never last.

<u>Uncap the Pen:</u>

Do you often live to please others more than live to do the things you're passionate about? Jot down a few of the things you would pursue if you had more time.

____

____

____

Now, list out two things you will do this week to get one step closer to your dream.

Could you wake up 15-30 minutes earlier to dedicate that time to your dream? Could you spend less time scrolling through social media to create extra time? How about the weekends? Could you wake up a little earlier instead of sleeping in? You don't have to start huge and dedicate twenty-five hours to it. Think of small, attainable steps you can take.

____

____

____

Why do you want to do this? Write yourself a reminder as to why you want to divorce the pattern of people-pleasing. When you go through challenging times and are tempted to fall back into this pattern, you can look back and reflect on your why.

____

____

____

____

____

____

<u>Sign the Divorce Papers:</u>

"Dear God, thank You for the talents, passions, and gifts You have blessed me with. I know I don't always use them to my fullest potential and that I often prioritize other things ahead of them, but I want to be better. I want to live my life to please You and not worry about disappointing or letting other people down. You gave me this life, and I want to live it for You. Shift my focus away from the buffet, and to the main dish that You have for me. Let my thoughts be filled with Your truth and not the lies of the enemy, guilting me into yet another unfulfilling commitment. Pile Your truths and Your direction, clarity, wisdom, understanding, and purpose onto my plate. When I sit at the table, I want my plate to be so full of Your love, grace, kindness, and mercy, that it flows onto the plates of others. Let there not only be enough for me but for every single person I encounter."

Partnering with Patience

*Let us not become weary in doing good, for at the proper
time we will reap a harvest if we do not give up.*
Galatians 6:9, NIV

Did you see the end of that sentence? IF we do not give up.
Hello to a very difficult thing to practice.

The truth is, we have become a society that has a hard time
waiting for anything. We market freaky fast deliveries and
yearn for overnight results. These stand in stark contrast
to requiring patience and perseverance. They, instead,
encourage compromise in our decisions.

That job you imagined you'd have right after college? You
need ten years experience.

The husband or wife you thought you'd be married to at age
twenty-three? Patience. He or she will be in your story at age
thirty-two.

The salary you thought you'd be earning by now to do the
things you've dreamed of doing but need the finances? It'll
come after you persevere through this job you dislike for five
years, and after you start trusting the Lord through tithing
at church. Throughout the years, you will learn. The lessons
and knowledge acquired will then lead to the bigger earnings
you anticipated.

The home with a cozy fireplace and the perfect view to watch
the sunset and sunrise every day you thought you'd create?
Not for fifteen years.

Don't we sometimes wish we could bargain with God? "Hey,
Lord . . . I know I'm not supposed to receive that raise, the
house, the marriage, the _______, for another two years, but
if I promise to pray every single day and go to church every

Marrying Freedom

Sunday, do You think You could speed it up?" That would be ideal! However, that's not how things work.

We will all go through seasons of waiting for different things – jobs, healing, a relationship, reconciliation, clarity, finances, the list goes on. I've been through my fair share of being patient for all of those things, and even more. How did I find comfort through it? I clung to God's Word. One of my favorite verses, when I'm faced with being patient for something, is found in Lamentations. I have leaned into this promise time and time again, "The Lord is good to those whose hope is in him, to the one who seeks him; it is good to wait quietly for the salvation of the Lord" (Lamentations 3:25-26, NIV). It's all for our good. If we haven't received the promise we are believing Him for, it's because we aren't ready for it.

If He gave us what we are hoping for right now, we might not have the capacity to excel in it, or we might not be ready to carry it out as He intends.

You want that job, but you don't yet have the skills necessary to accomplish what He needs you to in the position. He must first take you through this certain season to unmask qualities and skills in you that will differentiate you from the other candidates for the position. Because you waited and went through this season, you will accomplish far more. You are going to impact not just one life, but many lives because you waited and developed more as a person. He has such big plans ahead of you, an even brighter and more inspiring future than the one you're planning in your head.

You want the marriage, but you haven't developed a dependence on the Lord. If you were to get married right now, the spouse would become the idol of your life, rather than God being at the center of your marriage. You would let every single choice you make be centered on your spouse—causing you to steer clear from the things the Lord wants you to step into, which creates heavy anxiety and fear of disappointment in everything you do.

Partnering with Patience

You want to go to a specific college, but you don't want to take the time to do your homework and get good grades. You've taken to copying your friend's work, and you don't do so well on the tests, because you don't know what you're doing. You get upset when you begin to fail classes but learn that the Lord was drawing you somewhere completely different than where you had planned. Rather than a huge university, He's leading you to a community college, where you'll launch into activities you're passionate about, impacting various groups on campus.

Many of us don't want the journey. We don't want to have to be patient. We don't want to be told to be patient. We don't want to hear the words, "in God's timing." We want it all like we want our food: fast and convenient. Any process to attain the things we really want is dreaded. Can't we just order it up and have it overnight, or Amazon Prime that thing? There's overnight shipping, so can't we have overnight answered prayers? I mean, God can hear every single prayer and thought, so if He hears it, shouldn't He send some answers?

Throughout different seasons of waiting, I came to realize I was so focused on what I wanted, I didn't take a step back and consider whether it was what God wanted for me.

Are there things you've prayed for in the past you're thankful didn't get answered? For me, that's true. The things I thought were so good were not even comparable to what the Lord had and has in store for me.

The job I thought was the perfect fit? It drained me and made me into someone I didn't even recognize—highly stressed and short with loved ones.

The man I fell for quickly and was almost certain I was going to marry after just a few dates? Gone, after a one-sentence text, leaving my heart broken and yearning for closure that never came.

The friendship I thought would last forever? We haven't spoken in years.

If all of my prayers were answered, I would have been married a few times by now to the wrong guy. I'd be living somewhere across the country. I'd be working in a different field. I'd have a completely different life.

As we go through life, there are things that turn out differently than we had hoped or anticipated. There will be seasons where we think we're right where God wants us, yet a whole different story is unfolding, behind the scenes, that will change the trajectory of the future.

You don't know it yet, but you will, in His perfect timing. Sometimes, you know exactly what you're waiting for, and you know when it will come to pass. Graduation, a job promotion, the wedding date, the move. You know it's coming, but you can't fast forward to make it arrive any quicker. You're not crazy about waiting, but you know you have to until the set date arrives. Knowing the day, the season, or the timeframe makes waiting a little more manageable.

In God's plan and timing, we don't necessarily want to wait, but we know it's vital.

It can become very challenging to maintain a positive mindset through waiting, especially when you look around and see people attaining the very thing your heart is waiting and longing for.

The job. The restoration. The relationship. The marriage. The baby. The friendship. The vacation. The this, the that.

"Hello, Lord. Do you not hear my desperate pleas for this? Are you even listening?" I've said that many times. If I'm honest, I've prayed that quite a few times in the past few months.

Yes; I know He's working, but wouldn't it help sometimes if we could physically be assured of it? Why can't He give us some little progress bars so we can see how close or far away we are from the object of our anticipation? There's a situation I've been praying on for years, and there have been plenty of times I've doubted, become impatient, lost hope, tried to work it out on my own, and become so frustrated by it. Then, as He always does, He comes through with reassurance: "Hil, I'm here. I'm right behind you, and I'm working on it. I know it doesn't feel like it, and I know you're nervous and frustrated, but take heart. You might not see it now, but you will. Just keep trusting me. Just keep believing I will turn it for your good."

Maybe you're saying that same thing right now: "Are you even listening, Lord? Maybe you need to clean your ears out, God; have You tried that?"

He's listening, friend. He hears you. He sees you. He knows your heart, every ache, desire, and joy. He knows it inside and out, much better than you even know what your heart is feeling.

In 2019, I interviewed for a job in Los Angeles. Yes, LA, California. It's funny now, the thought of small-town, country-living me in the big city of LA.

I was utterly convinced this was the next step I was supposed to take. I'd felt the Lord was calling me to somewhere and something new, and it felt like everything was falling into place too easily for it not to be the next step.

The process began in February. I had four interviews within two weeks. They had gone REALLY well, and I knew that I was most likely going to get the job offer. I was both excited and terrified about what that meant. My friend worked for the same company and knew an apartment that was opening up within the month, which was the timeframe they were looking to fill the opening. It was an excellent price for rent in LA. To top it all off, it was just a few blocks from the beach and not too far from the office.

Wow, Lord. I'm moving to California.

The day in mid-March came when I received a phone call. It was the Talent Acquisition Manager, and she was calling to explain they had to put their hiring process on hold. They were waiting for approval to go through for their client, whose events I would be working on, and they couldn't hire without knowing they'd gotten that account back. They didn't want to hire someone and have them move across the country, to work a position that might not exist any longer.

However, the good news was, they knew the date the contract would go through if they got it back . . . April 19. She made it sound as if, once it went through, they were going to hire me. Basically, she said without saying it, the job was mine.

Okay, so a month . . . That'd give me time to get my things in order, enjoy time at home, and train the people at work. Because I was planning to leave, I was working fewer hours. I was ready and committed to this new opportunity.

The days flew by. I loved where I was, but I was continually nudged by God that it wasn't the right fit for me, and I was so excited about what was to come. There were moments of extreme hesitation and a lack of peace, but I figured this was because I was nervous about moving across the country. Every day, "something new, something unfamiliar" were the words God was laying heavily on my heart. Okay, yeah; California would be a HUGE move to somewhere completely unfamiliar for this back road-loving girl.

Well, April 19, arrived and passed. Still no word. About a week after that, I received an email from the HR woman, checking in to see how I was doing. She hadn't received any updates yet but wanted to stay in touch to make sure I wasn't moving forward elsewhere. A couple of weeks later, another email. Still no update.

Okay, God . . . What is this? Why is this opportunity, which seemed perfect and fell into place so easily, now becoming an extended process with no movement?

Partnering with Patience

As I began to take more time to pray about it and seek clarity and peace for the next step, I began putting in applications for other opportunities. Maybe this wasn't the correct next step for me. I'd been so set on getting out of Illinois, but maybe the new He was leading me to wasn't across the country. Maybe it meant something new right where I was. My focus shifted to writing, to be more present where I was, still keeping an eye out for different opportunities.

I kept getting the sense that "something new" was coming, but nothing was coming to fruition. The more I prayed about it and had interviews in different parts of the country, the more uneasy I felt about moving away. I didn't want to stay. I wanted to experience life outside of Illinois, but I sensed God had other plans for me.

As I was preparing for an interview for a position in Kentucky, I closed my eyes and said a prayer. I asked for clarity and for the Lord to give me the vision to see the next step, for some direction to Illinois or elsewhere. I flipped open my devotion for that day. The first sentence of that page?

"You are right where you are supposed to be."

Okay, God. Well, not what I was hoping for, but if this is indeed where you want me, then I'll stay.

I had the interview and never heard anything back. A week later, things fell into place, and I finalized plans to partner with a friend and begin working on a few big projects right where I was. I attended a meeting that Wednesday, to begin planning for an event that was in the works. The more I learned about the project and what we'd be doing, the higher my level of excitement became. It was for a cause bigger than myself, and I was pumped to be a part of it.

I've always heard people talk about God's ironic timing, and He sure has a sense of humor alright.

Thursday morning, the NEXT day after finalizing the project

details, I was driving to work, when my phone began to ring. It was the HR lady from the job in LA. Now remember, the whole interview process began in February, and it's now mid-June.

Yes, four months. I hadn't heard from her in over a month, and the last time she checked in to see how I was doing, she still had no new updates.

"This is going to be completely out of left field, but we just got the approval to hire, and they'd like to offer you the job in LA."

You. Have. Got. To. Be. Kidding. Me. Lord.

The job I was convinced a few months ago I would take without hesitating, I was now turning down without even taking time to think about it. A job. Full-time. Benefits. With travel. What was I thinking?!

Well, in the season of waiting, God was revealing a different plan and giving me the season He knew I needed. Through having to be patient, I was given time to evaluate myself and dig deeper into what He was calling me to do. It was then I realized, by taking that job, no matter how awesome it would be, I'd simply be running away from what I knew He wanted me to do. I'd be running away from being present where I was, from the things He'd laid on my heart. I was trying to justify all of the reasons why I should go when I knew He wanted me to stay right where I was.

It was easy to turn it down, but at the same time, it wasn't. I wondered what experiences, travel, and new friendships I would miss out on. However, I felt a sense of peace that it was the right thing to do. It didn't stop with peace; I felt relief and excitement alongside it. I had been so set on moving, on being somewhere new, beginning a life elsewhere.

When I committed to being present where I was, I became excited. Rather than resenting and dreading the day-to-day, my soul beamed at all of the possibilities to make a difference right where I was.

As it turned out, my next step was somewhere completely new, doing something completely different, but it was in the same town. My friend called me one day and said, "There's this job opening where I work, and I think you'd be perfect for it." It wasn't something I was even going to consider, until I felt God's quiet whisper, "Don't turn it down right away. At least learn a little more." All it took was one meeting to know it was right where He wanted me.

I knew He had something good. It just took a whole lot of trust. I learned to surrender my future and plans to Him one day, one moment at a time.

Looking back, it was four months of preparation. Four months is nothing compared to the forty years Moses spent in the wilderness. God could have sped that time up. He could have made things fall into place sooner or let them stay where they were until it was time to lead his people to the Promised Land, but He didn't. He led them out, and then they waited. They faced trials and struggles. And then, they waited some more.

The Lord heard you when you wailed, "If only we had meat to eat! We were better off in Egypt!" Now the Lord will give you meat, and you will eat it. You will not eat it for just one day, or two days, or five, ten or twenty days, but for a whole month—until it comes out of your nostrils and you loathe it—because you have rejected the Lord, who is among you, and have wailed before him, saying, "Why did we ever leave Egypt?
Numbers 11:18-20, NIV

They didn't get what they expected or wanted right away, so we see them continue to complain. They spoke against God and against Moses, and said, "Why have you brought us up out of Egypt to die in the wilderness? There is no bread! There is no water! And we detest this miserable food" (Numbers 21:5,

NIV). Yet, Moses remained patient and pleaded with God for them. The Lord was teaching them to trust Him through the trials. He wanted to show them no matter what they faced, He would surround and protect them. He was there through the plagues and the hunger and directed their steps to the Promised Land in His perfect timing. Even though Moses wouldn't enter, he continued to show them patience and never left them through the journey.

God used that season for preparation, just as He uses our deserts and unappealing dry seasons to ready us. Without those four months of anticipating the move to California, I wouldn't have been ready for the responsibilities that lay ahead. Minus the skills, meetings, interactions, and learning in that season, I wouldn't have what I need to carry out the present day. In every single thing I've waited for, the wait has always been well worth it.

If you're in a season of waiting right now, instead of dreading and despising the time that is passing, try viewing it instead as preparation. Think of it like this: You're a seed ready to be planted. The field has to be prepared for planting. Once the seed is planted, it has to receive adequate rain and sunshine to grow. The seed must take root and turn into a plant over a period of time. It cannot be harvested too soon. The farmer must be patient until it is ready.

You are a seed. You will soon grow and flourish as a mom, an employee, a significant other, or a friend. You will blossom into an abundant crop, but you must partner with God in patience. Know that He is working to prepare you, to nourish you, to give you the sun, rain, and clouds that you need to grow into a ready-to-harvest crop. This requires waiting—and waiting well. Seek Him each and every day. Pray for discernment, that you walk into each day with eyes to see what He needs you to do. Serve those around you. Learn something new. Embrace the season. Find beauty in the little things. We often think our timing is much better, but we must learn to pause in His presence, no matter the period of time we must hold the pause.

Partnering with Patience

In His perfect timing, He will bring His promises to pass. The result might be what you were expecting, or it might contrast starkly with what you had in mind. Regardless, He will strengthen you, mold you, and provide you with everything you need. God will do what He needs to. He will prepare you so you can accomplish everything He has planned. Take heart. The crop is well worth the late nights and early mornings of planting, waiting, and harvesting. Just keep going with patience and perseverance, and keep sowing—God will continue to add to your efforts. He sees your work and takes note, nothing you do is unnoticed!

Uncap the Pen:

What are you waiting for right now? Are there plans you're anxiously awaiting? List them out below.

____

____

____

Has this been a short or long season of waiting? Have you learned anything so far in the wait?

____

____

____

What is something you can do while you wait that will better prepare you for what's ahead?

____

____

____

List some ways God has been faithful and come through for you in the past. Reflect on these when you get frustrated, discouraged, or tired of waiting.

____

____

____

<u>Sign the Divorce Papers:</u>

"Lord, this season seems like it is dragging on. My heart longs for so much more, but I know, trust, and believe that Your timing is perfect. Help me believe that You are preparing me for the future You have in store. Help me to be in the here and now, to be present where I am and where You have me, so I do not waste this season. God, I know there is a reason for everything. I know there is a great purpose in waiting, in being patient. I know the plans You have for me surpass anything my mind can conceive. Give my heart the peace and strength it needs to fully believe and surrender my timeline to You. You are greater, Your plans are greater, and Your love is greater than anything on this side of heaven. All I want to do is worship You throughout my life. Let the steps I take and the words I say all be reflective of You. Let my heart be open to the possibilities in front of me so that I will step into them with courage, even if it looks different than I thought it would. Help me to step exactly where You want me to step. I know the best is yet to come, so help me believe, learn, and pursue what you have for me. In Jesus' name."

Prevailing Over Perfection

*Indeed, there is no one on earth who is righteous,
no one who does what is right and never sins.
Ecclesiastes 7:20, NIV*

How many times do you take a photo before it's *just right*? How many angles, filters, and changes do you make to it before you feel it's okay to share for the rest of the world to see?

When you head out of the door, how many times do you glance in the mirror before you go? How many times do you change your outfit or hair, apply some makeup, trim up your beard, or check your brows?

As children, we used to live with simplicity in our daily lives. We lived without stress and drama and shrugged off the opinions of others. Somewhere along the way, we lost that. We became consumed with what people think or say about us. We started to feel the pressure to meet those expectations day after day.

The thing is, we were the ones to put those burdens on ourselves. We've convinced ourselves that we must be perfect. We tend to forget we're all human beings with real feelings and emotions. We face difficult seasons. We get zits, blemishes, rashes, hives, cold sores, poison ivy, or other things that make us self-conscious. We face challenges, highs, and lows.

We strive for the perfect test score.

We clean the entire house right before the company arrives for a visit.

On a work project, we obsess over the tiny details and comb through them ten times before submitting.

I think we tend to forget others also have imperfections and don't always have it all together.

The influencer with three kiddos, does not always have a mess-free home. The entrepreneur faces challenges, hard times, and late nights, even though he shows his booming businesses daily.

We forget about the journey it takes to accomplish something when viewing the edited highlight reels on social media. We see their "perfect" lives and convince ourselves we must meet and exceed the perfect standard shown online by our family and friends.

While social media can be a great tool to stay connected with people, it seems what it's become is far from what the Lord wants for us. It's not about staying connected anymore. Rather, it's become a tool we use to judge how worthy and likable our lives are. We start to base our value and worth on how many likes a photo gets, or how much engagement and shares a video receives.

The need to feel and appear perfect has only heightened with this shift. We see everyone's highlight reels in their posts. We start to question ourselves and wonder, *"Why in the world don't I have my life together? What's wrong with me?"*

The problem with this outlook is social media is not typically featuring behind-the-scenes, outtakes, or redos. It's not showing the raw, real, and true aspects of life—the blood, sweat, and tears. It's what people want others to see. It's them looking their best, in the best moments, with the best people at the best places.

It's not the husband, lying awake all night because of the fight he had with his wife.

It's not the woman, dripping with sweat from the hour-long workout, her hair a mess, with no makeup on.

It's not the parents spanking their child because he threw

Prevailing Over Perfection

food at the table next to them at the restaurant.

No.

It's the picture-perfect photo of the couple on a fancy date.

It's the abs and toned arms, sipping on the perfectly nutritious green smoothie.

It's the family on a vacation positioned right in front of the most popular state landmark.

It's exactly what each individual wants the rest of the world to see. It was likely a created scenario, carefully planned out. Intentional. Crafted.

It looks perfect; the preset made the lighting just right. They used the auto-correct feature and the latest filter. It appears flawless.

However, this is where we are all wrong. We think it looks perfect, but we forget that perfection can't ever be attained. Not a single soul on this planet is perfect. No family, relationship, job, or friendship is impeccable. Since the time of Adam and Eve, we're born into a fallen world; hence, nothing on this side of heaven will ever be completely one-hundred percent flawless. Things in our lives will always ebb and flow.

There might be moments that *feel* perfect. There might be times when things **seem** perfect, yet this will be only a glimpse of perfection. The here and now is fleeting. Only when we meet our Maker will we experience what perfection truly is. We are reminded of this by a man named Solomon. He tested a variety of scenarios, and did he find perfection in any of them? No. Instead, he was reminded of the vanity of life and how satisfaction is only found in Christ.

> *I said to myself, "Come now, I will test you with pleasure*
> *to find out what is good." But that also proved to be*

meaningless. "Laughter," I said, "is madness. And what does pleasure accomplish?" I tried cheering myself with wine, and embracing folly—my mind still guiding me with wisdom. I wanted to see what was good for people to do under the heavens during the few days of their lives.

I undertook great projects: I built houses for myself and planted vineyards. I made gardens and parks and planted all kinds of fruit trees in them. I made reservoirs to water groves of flourishing trees. I bought male and female slaves and had other slaves who were born in my house. I also owned more herds and flocks than anyone in Jerusalem before me. I amassed silver and gold for myself, and the treasure of kings and provinces. I acquired male and female singers, and a harem as well—the delights of a man's heart. I became greater by far than anyone in Jerusalem before me. In all this my wisdom stayed with me.

I denied myself nothing my eyes desired; I refused my heart no pleasure. My heart took delight in all my labor, and this was the reward for all my toil. Yet when I surveyed all that my hands had done and what I had toiled to achieve, everything was meaningless, a chasing after the wind; nothing was gained under the sun.
Ecclesiastes 2:4-11, NIV

Do you see all of the projects he worked on and the desires he fulfilled? Yet, nothing was gained from it. If he tried it all out, can't we be certain of one thing? Nothing on this side of heaven will fill us. The things we strive for, trying to create a picture-perfect image? They're never going to be perfect. Many times, things won't turn out how we expected or planned. If they do, the feeling or the impression it leaves on others is only temporary. Solomon himself reminds us of this. We know this, so why do we put so much pressure on ourselves that we need to have it all together and appear so to those around us?

We either strive for perfection or we're stuck, paralyzed by the fear of trying and failing, for standing out, for trying something new. You might be trying to accomplish something, but you've been battling some opposition. You've hit a few rough patches and don't know how it's going to turn out. You've been hard on yourself and beating yourself up about it. You have to remember: it's okay to mess up! Use the flops as a learning experience. Don't become defeated because you think you have to get it right on the first try. This is how we all grow, through trial and error! Grow forward! Failing at something doesn't mean you're weak. It means you're human. You've got this! Don't give up.

It's okay to be vulnerable about your imperfections and shortcomings. It's okay to share about the things in your life that have been less than perfect. Now, I'm not saying you should do that with every person you come across, but don't shut out the rest of the world if there's something going on in your life that might make you appear as someone with struggles, because, guess what? We all have them!

Sometimes sharing the challenges we're going through can be the catalyst for someone going through something similar. It could help bring about healing and instill encouragement, hope, restoration, and peace. We have no idea what good it could do to those who hear. We have to remember we are not alone. We all have things that are far from perfect, though we wish or try to portray that they are.

I never used to be too quiet about what was going on in my life. I'd share about what I was doing and what I was struggling with. Really, anything anyone wanted to know, they could ask, and I'd tell. I was an open book.

Somewhere along the road, it all shifted. I watched people I cared for getting burned by someone they loved. I saw people misuse the information to destroy others, and others told me they had been praying for the exact opposite of what I had asked them to pray.

So, I became extremely introverted with all of my information, put on a tough face, and anywhere I went, I made sure

Marrying Freedom

I looked strong, even if I was a mess and something was breaking me. I created the impression I was happy. I put on a mask I wouldn't take off for anyone.

Rather than being an open book, I'm very careful with what I talk about and who I share it with. Maybe it's fear of what they will think, or perhaps I'm afraid they'll try to manipulate me or do something terrible if they learn of a weakness or flaw. It could be if they know I have real problems going on in my life—even though everyone does—then, they'll look at me differently. Many people haven't heard the stories in this book, so when I contemplated sharing some of them, I had to overcome the fear of caring what others would think or say upon reading it.

No, I'm not perfect.
Yes, I struggle, just like you.
Yes, I've had my heart broken more than once.
Yes, I change my clothes and check the mirror too many times before leaving home.
Yes, I put makeup on to cover up zits and tired eyes.
Yes, I make mistakes.
Yes, I am sometimes too concerned with other people's thoughts and opinions of me.

I'm not perfect, and I don't try to be.

Just a few weeks ago, I had my first experience with poison oak. I'd never had anything like that, and it just so happened I got it in the most visible places—on my neck, chin, and eyes.

Did I mention those are extremely visible places?

My thoughts towards myself during those weeks were not kind. My eyes were swollen and itched like crazy. Two cracks decided to appear on my lips, which resulted in a cold sore . . . the cherry on top.

I refrained from applying much makeup to eliminate aggravation. One day, within an hour of being at work, three different people came into my office asking what was wrong with my face. I chuckled it off, but deep down, I hated those few weeks. I didn't like people being hyper-aware of my appearance. I didn't want people asking me day after day what was wrong with me.

I knew they didn't mean anything by it, but man . . . After so many questions about it, it started to get to me. One day, we were on our way to church, and I was so frustrated after looking in the mirror before we left the house. I hated my appearance and how the poison oak was making me feel about myself. I threw a little pity party, left our apartment in a down mood, and ended up crying in the car.

My husband was a tad surprised by this because having poison oak wasn't the biggest deal or the end of the world, and he gently reminded me it would be gone before I knew it.

Yes, I knew that, BUT that reassurance didn't help in the present moment. I had been taken down the rabbit hole of facing imperfection head-on. In person, I couldn't apply a filter or hide what was in plain sight, and the impact it had on me was more painful than I would like to admit.

I was oh so humbly reminded that God never promised us life would be perfect. He didn't create us to be perfect or to look perfect. He didn't design us with the most flawless skin that never gets rashes or swollen. He doesn't want us to blend in and do what everyone else is doing. He didn't order us to live without making mistakes or having flaws. He knows that's unrealistic. He knew, from the very start, we wouldn't be perfect, so why are we putting this pressure on ourselves?

He created you with a unique and special purpose that might require some trial and error, learning and discovering, rashes and frustrations, and failures and successes. He didn't create you to sit comfy in your latest job because you're financially secure yet bored to death, using none of your passions or talents. He created you for more.

Someone told me recently, "Don't be afraid to make mistakes. Don't be afraid to fail."

Don't we live quite the opposite? We're terrified to take a chance, to take a risk, to do something that would stand out from the crowd because we're scared silly of messing up and other people seeing it. We think we can find happiness only by being perfect. How far from the truth is that?!

We need to kick that thinking to the curb. We need more rawness, more risk-taking, and more seeing ourselves as God sees us. We need to step into the life God has for us and live in it confidently, no matter how "silly" we look to others. It's time to prevail over that idea of perfection.

No matter what other people think of us, God sees each and every one of us as perfect. We don't have to strive to be something we're not. We don't have to cover up who we are to fit in. We don't have to spend two hours getting ready to go somewhere. We don't have to be loaded with money, capable of buying anything our heart desires. Every piece of who we are is exactly how He created us.

We won't get into heaven based on what others think or what we can buy. We won't find freedom in any of our possessions or what we portray our life to be. Rather, Jesus reminds us, "If you want to be perfect, go, sell your possessions and give to the poor, and you will have treasure in heaven. Then come, follow me" (Matthew 19:21, NIV).

He doesn't say, "Go, take five photos, put a filter on the best one, post it at the prime time, while all of your followers are online, then come follow me." There are no regulations that you have to be 100% ready. There are no boxes you have to check off before you can come to Him. He doesn't say you have to have it all together to follow Him. You don't have to earn His approval or love. He doesn't even say you have to bring anything along; instead, He says to sell all of your possessions. You can come to Him empty-handed.

Prevailing Over Perfection

Can you imagine if we lived with this abandon in our lives? Wow. We would be so rich!

What would it look like if we moved with this intention? Can we start to live with the realization that Jesus sees and knows our hearts? He knows what we think, the words we speak, the things that cause us deep pain and frustration, and the circumstances that leave us feeling a little down. He sees us when we're put together and when we're falling apart. Still, He loves us . . . THE MOST. He thinks you are perfect. He loves you the most of anything He created.

He promised, "And everyone who has left houses or brothers or sisters or father or mother or wife or children or fields for my sake will receive a hundred times as much and will inherit eternal life" (Matthew 19:29, NIV).

A hundred times as much. Don't you want to walk in that freedom, abundance, and love? Let us no longer strive for perfection but, instead, work on persisting and prevailing when things aren't 100% perfect. Let's embrace the truth that all you are and all you give is enough. Don't be afraid of making mistakes, of failing, or of other people's opinions.

His love is perfect, and in His eyes, no matter how imperfect you feel, you are loved, and you are perfect. No matter what the rest of the world tells you, there is no filter, no auto-tuning you need to do. You don't have to work for it, edit it, or request it. His love for you is freely given, right as you are: blemishes, insecurities, fears, and all.

Uncap the Pen:

In what areas of your life do you try to appear perfect? Your work life? Family life? Finances? Friendships? Fitness?

____

____

____

What is the reasoning behind why you work to create a certain image for others? Is it to impress them? To seem put together? Think about your why, and write it out below.

____

____

____

What is one of your struggles you feel could help someone, if you were more vulnerable, raw, and real about what you've been through or what you're going through?

____

____

____

Sign the Divorce Papers:

"Lord, You didn't create me to be perfect. I know that nothing on this earth will ever be perfect, yet I strive to create that image on a daily basis. I know I have shortcomings, and I know everyone around me does too. Help me to be more raw and real. Help me to share with others what I am struggling with, removing all fear of judgment or condemnation for it.

Prevailing Over Perfection

Remind me frequently that what I see online is oftentimes the highlight reel, not the real and raw moments. When I fall into the pit, help me remember that social media is simply an image being planned and created intentionally. God, there is no filter on Your love. Help me to love that same way. Instill in my heart the compassion You have for others, to see them and love them right where they are. You are so good, and this life You've given me is so good. I know it doesn't have to be perfect for it to be amazing. Give me a heart of gratitude for whatever this life holds. You are perfect, and Your ways are perfect. I pray to step into the plans You have for me and glorify Your name in all that I do, share, think, and say."

Cultivating Contentment

But godliness with contentment is great gain. For we brought nothing into the world, and we can take nothing out of it.
1 Timothy 6:6-7, NIV

I'll be happy
When ... I get the promotion.
When ... I get married.
When ... I have a child.
When ... I'm in a relationship.
When ... I go out with my friends.
When ... I take a vacation.
When ... I purchase this new appliance for my home.
When ... I lose 20 pounds.

What's your when?

We all have things we hope for and want in our lives. Having desires isn't a bad thing. Setting goals and working to achieve them, then seeing them come to pass, is an awesome feeling and accomplishment. Having some sort of direction is needed for us to grow. Otherwise, we would remain stagnant, never changing or improving.

Goals are great, but when these items of focus begin to consume us and become our top priority, that's when we lose our peace. We become convinced we will only be happy once we have _______ (insert your *when*).

More often than not, I see and hear people attain their desire, only to have it replaced with something else. Then, the cycle begins again.

I have this job; now I can't wait to get a promotion.
I have this awesome coffee maker that will make lattes; Now, all I need is a fireplace to sit by to enjoy my coffee. I need a

bigger house with more space.
I have a car that works, but boy, I can't wait to purchase a newer one with better gadgets and an automatic start.
I'm on this exotic, warm vacation with my loved ones, but I want to go to this place where this other family on Facebook just posted. Look how cool it looks!

It becomes a chain of want, want, want. When will our hearts be content? Will they ever?

The truth is, we have more than enough, yet we live in a constant state of not having enough. If I asked you out of the blue, what's one thing you want right now, you'd probably have no problem rattling off a whole list. I agree. I could do it myself.

Whether it's a want or a need, there will always be at least one item at the top of the list. How do we determine if those things on our dockets are costing us our contentment, or if they're motivators to do better and be better?

Our goals and aspirations steal our freedom when they consume our hearts, minds, and souls, when they become our sole focus. Our addiction. We find ourselves attaining thing after thing yet keep striving for more. We discover we are not content once we attain the object of our fantasy.

We all live with a void inside of us. It's a void that cannot ever be filled, yet we try. We pursue the latest iPhone, the bigger lake house, sex, drugs, money, pornography, alcohol, the classiest apartment, new cars, boats, properties, gear, or the latest items that all the commercials are marketing.

Don't we experience a rush, a sense of fulfillment, or success when we receive or participate in some of those things? When we reach a goal we've been working on? We feel the flow of power that comes with it, and we crave more. For a moment, we are full. But more times than not, the sensation is fleeting and the cycle continues. We become desperate to feel it again. It costs us our freedom. It locks us into the continual, never-ending cycle of more, more, more. We think to ourselves: If I just have *this*, then others will think I have made it. If I just buy *that*, I will finally be happy.

Are you content, though? What happens when that goal, the money, a desired item, is in your possession? Does it make you feel on top of the world? Do you feel valuable? Do you feel confident and proud of how you are able to satisfy your every desire because you can buy whatever you need to feel whole, if only temporarily? Does the way you achieved that goal make you feel good about yourself, or are you ashamed but block out those sentiments?

If, after some reflection, you've realized your peace is conditioned to completing and achieving the items on your checklists, it's time to rework your thinking!

How can we fill that void and cultivate contentment with where we are and with what we have? How do we learn to experience peace and gratitude in every season?

We can learn an important lesson from Solomon. One night, the Lord appeared to him in a dream and told him to ask for whatever he wanted the Lord to give him.

Your servant is here among the people you have chosen, a great people, too numerous to count or number. So give your servant a discerning heart to govern your people and to distinguish between right and wrong. For who is able to govern this great people of yours?"

The Lord was pleased that Solomon had asked for this. So God said to him, "Since you have asked for this and not for long life or wealth for yourself, nor have asked for the death of your enemies but for discernment in administering justice, I will do what you have asked. I will give you a wise and discerning heart, so that there will never have been anyone like you, nor will there ever be. Moreover, I will give you what you have not asked for—both wealth and honor— so that in your lifetime you will have no equal among kings.
1 Kings 3:8-13, NIV

He could have asked for anything. The Lord himself asked him what he wanted. Yet, all Solomon asked for was to have a discerning heart. Rather than pursuing more and more riches, He pursued God. He showed gratitude for what he had and enjoyed his life. It didn't stop with him. Those around him benefited as well. Word of his wisdom spread throughout the region and came to the ears of the queen of Sheba.

She ventured to him with a large entourage to visit. She spoke everything that was on her mind and asked him many difficult questions, but he had the wisdom to respond and answer every one. Seeing all he had built and accomplished astounded her.

She told him,

"I didn't believe what was said until I arrived here and saw it with my own eyes. In fact, I had not heard the half of your great wisdom! It is far beyond what I was told. How happy your people must be! What a privilege for your officials to stand here day after day, listening to your wisdom"
2 Chronicles 9:6-7, NLT

He could have asked for anything, but he sought the Lord and His counsel. This wisdom didn't only help him but everyone who came into contact with him. Can you imagine being led by someone who is guided by the Lord, every day, in every decision? Guess what? We can be a leader like that to those around us! We can shift our focus from the things of this world, to Jesus. He's our Creator, and He's the fulfiller of every desire and every need we'll ever require.

It will be hard. Our society puts success and money on a pedestal. Millions of marketing dollars are spent every year highlighting products that we need. What people have forgotten is these items will never satisfy and money will never purchase us true happiness and fulfillment. However, we've been taught to believe it will. As a result, we work and sell and do everything we can to bring in more and more money. We sometimes forget what's written right in the Bible: "The love of money is a root of all kinds of evil. Some people, eager for money, have wandered from the faith and pierced themselves with many griefs" (1 Timothy 6:10, NIV).

Yes, money can be used for good; it can help people in need. It buys food and supplements and everything we need. But, it can also cause destruction. It can create a wedge in a relationship; it can destroy families. It can cause people to turn into someone they're not, simply because of their desire for control of it. It says right there in the Bible that it can pierce people with many griefs. I've seen money and greed absolutely destroy families, relationships, and friendships, and it's the most heartbreaking thing.

Money talks, and it doesn't say anything nice when it's used for the wrong reasons. If it had a conversation bubble for what it was saying, it surely would be terms we couldn't mention here. It doesn't say anything nice because it's not what our hearts were designed to crave. It's not what we were created to seek and pursue, yet it often competes for our contentment. Earthly possessions and money are not what we were created for, yet people have become slaves to them.

Having more money becomes the sole intention and desire in life for some. It becomes so important that it doesn't matter what has to be done to obtain more. It's a wicked cycle that takes down more homes in America than fires. Rather than finding peace and contentment with the accumulation of wealth, it turns into a vicious cycle of craving more, that never stops burning.

Will you be the one to take a stand against it? Will you get out your fire extinguisher and put out the blaze? Will you work on cultivating contentment or cave to your craving? You may find yourself living an enriched life, but are you being a blessing to others through it, or are you simply using it to boast about your belongings? Rather than showing your appreciation to God, are you scurrying after the next physical item you can get your hands on?

When I was a child, my wants were more for physical items: a new Barbie, a new book, or a new clothing piece. It became a competition at Christmastime between classmates about who received the best and most things. I remember receiving phone calls from some of them to ask what we had gotten for Christmas ... on Christmas Day! Those things we received would lose their sparkle in just a few weeks. We'd forget about them and go on to play with the next toy, the next game. They weren't things that were life-giving; they were just that—things.

As I've gotten older, it's become so much less about the physical items and more about the intangible items: peace, joy, happiness, fulfillment, family, and friends that point me to Jesus. For, those around me have the opportunity to know who Christ is; that strangers on the street, and those I run into at the grocery store, know the promise of eternal life at the end of their journeys. Being blessed, so I can be a blessing.

Things are fleeting; they can be stolen, bought, sold, and ruined. They come into style, and they go out of style. They can mold, age, and be affected by the weather. They are fragile, and, in seconds, can be demolished, destroyed, or lost. Nothing on this side of heaven is permanent, yet we're living like it'll affect us in a permanent fashion if we do not get it.

Our God is the opposite. His Word always stands true. His character is unchanging, yet there will be times when we feel there is a void in our life. We may feel empty, as if we're lacking something, or maybe we go through bouts of loneliness. We search for meaning and a way to fill those voids. We think it can be satisfied by purchasing or obtaining something physical. We seek after it, day after day, buying more *things*. What we tend to forget is nothing we can see or buy will ever satisfy. It's the Lord and His love, strength, and fulfillment that our hearts crave and desire. We were created in the image of God, and our completeness comes from His design. Only then, when we seek Him, when we grow in our relationship with Jesus and live with an attitude of gratitude, our hearts will feel peace, our desires met, and our nature will feel full.

If you don't already, start practicing gratitude every single day. A while back, I heard of a gratitude journal where you list things each day that you are grateful for. I thought it was such a great idea, and it's something I have implemented into my daily journal time. It can be anything, big or small: a job promotion, a roof over your head, shoes on your feet, the health of a loved one, breath in your lungs. Anything. List it. Find a new appreciation for the blessings God has bestowed in your life.

What if you think you have nothing to be grateful for? Well, you are reading this book, so that means two things: you are alive, and you have the resources to buy this, or you have someone who cares for you in your life who gifted it to you. Sometimes it's so easy to fix our eyes on what we don't have, that it becomes a challenge to appreciate what is right in front of us.

When you are grateful, then generosity will sprout from you. When you practice gratitude, your mindset and outlook are a little different, and your character is a little more open to looking around, rather than within. Are there needs around you? In what ways could you help? Have you ever considered how being generous outside of you can lead to fulfillment within you? This will honor not only the person you're serving but God as well. You'll find yourself with an overflowing heart.

When he asked for wisdom, this decision didn't only impact Solomon. It had a ripple effect and spread far and wide. He impacted countless lives. You have the opportunity to do the same.

There will always be things that will catch your eye and attention. There will be items and goals that distract you from God. He knows we're craving more out of this world. He simply desires our hearts and our time. He won't stop chasing after us. Just as we chase after things, He's after our hearts. It's His love and relationship that we need, and it won't be until we fix our eyes on Jesus and let Him be our fulfillment that we will be truly satisfied.

Uncap the Pen:

Take a look at your life. Do you live your days in want of the next thing, the next accessory, the hottest gadget, your next vacation? Try to be more aware of your cravings throughout your day. Tonight, list the things you noticed yourself saying, "I want __________."

____

____

____

Did you notice that you stated your desires aloud, or did you not say them at all? Were these items physical things you will purchase or things that could never be bought?

____

____

____

Cultivating Contentment

Why do you think you desire the things you listed above? For yourself? Your family? To create an image for others?

____

____

____

Next time you find yourself wanting something, choose to, instead, be grateful. Find something from the day you are thankful for, and focus on that. Create a list of things in your life you are thankful for today. Let gratitude overwhelm your soul and lead you to contentment in any and all situations.

____

____

____

Sign the Divorce Papers:

"Lord, I know You give and take away all things in this life. Whether painful or easy, You are there, every step of the way, and there is a great reason for it all. Help me find peace and contentment in whatever it is You have for me. Help me walk in confidence with the blessings, passions, people, and places You've given me. Curb the desires of my heart so they are focused on You and what You want for me. Fill the spaces in my heart that I try to satisfy with things of the world, and overwhelm me instead with fulfillment found in You. You are all I need; help me to realize and remember that when I find myself seeking the world more than I seek You. You're all I want and all I need. Let that be the anthem of my life."

Marrying Freedom

Winning the Wrestle with Worry

Therefore do not worry about tomorrow, for tomorrow will worry about itself. Each day has enough trouble of its own.
Matthew 6:34, NIV

If you watch the nightly news for just the first five minutes, you're likely to get up from your spot on the couch feeling a little unsafe and worried. Another shooting. A break-in. A robbery. A stabbing. A kidnapping. A fire. Storms. Tornados. Devastation. For the past years, COVID. Presidential elections. Yowzers.

The uplifting news stories are far and few. If anything, it's often a little two-minute segment fit in right at the end. You gotta finish on a positive note, right?

Well, the other twenty-eight minutes are enough to cast you into a chain of what-ifs that will keep you up all night. There is so much bad going on in the world, and every day it seems to become even more of a scary place full of awful happenings.

Filling your mind with the world's news, multiple times each day or week, can do some serious damage, especially if you already have a problem of being a worry wart.

Maybe you think I'm crazy, but I never watch the news. Sure, I might not be aware of every single thing happening in the world, but if something super important is happening that I do need to know about, I'm sure it'll come up across my computer screen, social media feeds, or through someone at work. If I need to know it, I will hear about it somehow, somewhere.

I used to thrive on anxiety. If there was something to worry about, I had it covered. Simply give me a little information about an unsettling situation, and I was in worry mode. Over time, I learned putting myself in situations that cause me to get anxious can be avoided. While I certainly can't control things that happen in the world around me, I can filter what I allow into my ears and mind.

No, the news doesn't make me anxious but hearing or viewing so much bad news doesn't do me any good. I'm sure you've heard the saying who and what you surround yourself with you become. Likewise, what you allow into your mind, you will eventually come to believe and abide by, because you continually filter it in.

Let's compare it to our morning cup of coffee. The thoughts we think are the coffee grounds. We add the water, turn on our coffee maker, and it begins to do its work. It filters the grounds and makes us a big, tasty cup of coffee. But what happens when those grounds are moldy or have a flavor we dislike? It comes out as a cup full of coffee we want to dump down the sink. Our negative thoughts are the moldy grounds. We don't want to put that in our cup and snuggle up on the couch to drink it. No, we're getting rid of it as fast as we can and replacing it with something we enjoy. What if we looked at our thought patterns and what we focused on in the same manner? Focus on the positive, good things, and we'll have fresher coffee, brighter thoughts, and less worry.

Can you become more aware and start to filter where your mind wanders and what you allow into your ears and eyes? By fixating on all of the bad news and awful tragedies, your mind is going to go there, no matter your situation.

Perhaps you think of the story you heard recently about tourists who were kidnapped as your family departs for a vacation.

Maybe you think of a story of a woman murdered at a rest stop as your family travels by car.

When you send your child off to school, you're paralyzed by fear as you think of the school shootings that are becoming more rampant.

Winning the Wrestle with Worry

When you're worshiping at church, you think of the man that entered a service and shot innocent members.

I think we can all relate to the coronavirus pandemic. I remember when it was first in the news. We were en route to San Diego for a family vacation. It crossed our minds, but we didn't have any worries about it. We flew there, enjoyed the trip, and came back home. Nothing seemed out of the ordinary. It was on TV, but the airports, car rentals, and everyone we saw were living their normal lives.

About one month after our return, everything hit the fan. Businesses were ordered to close. Schools forced e-learning. States declared "stay-at-home" orders. Limits were placed on the number of people permitted in the grocery store or at family gatherings. All we heard were headlines of hospital admission and death rates. If we turned on the news for five minutes, we were, more than likely, going to convince ourselves not to leave our house until all of it was over.

I was at work one day, shortly after everything shut down, and, having the label of "essential workers," we were still fulfilling obligations at the office throughout the pandemic. One of my coworkers mentioned she was so tired because she stayed up past eleven the night before. It wasn't because she was watching a movie or her favorite show but because she couldn't stop watching the news. She iterated how scary everything was. As I was leaving that afternoon, I said to her, "Do not turn on the news tonight, and do not stay up all night watching it again."

Now call me naive, but throughout the whole pandemic, I avoided watching the news at all costs. I knew my employer, my family, or my friends would share any vital information I needed to know. There was no need for me to see the daily death rate ticker, how many people were in the ER in New York City, and the shortages the country was experiencing for protective equipment. I knew it could and would provoke anxiety inside of me, so the TV remained off. I was on social media quite a bit at the beginning of it all, and after scrolling through and seeing post after post about it, I never felt a sense of comfort. I found myself terrified of getting sick.

I'd wake up with a slight cough from the dry air in my apartment and wonder if I was getting COVID-19.

In the middle of the night, I'd feel a little toasty from sleeping under my weighted blanket, and question if I had a fever.

If I felt the slightest runny nose, I smelled something every five minutes to make sure I could still smell and taste.

Worry. The worry was doing absolutely nothing good for me, and, not to mention, worry isn't the greatest for your immune system, either.

I limited social media and turned to the Word. Boy oh boy, did I feel better just by making that little switch. Rather than succumbing to the fear instilled by the news, I was struck by promises of hope and deliverance for those that partnered with the Lord.

I began to realize things could be fine one minute, then completely different the next. Times like that can throw us into a frenzy. We're not alone in those moments, and there have been people for thousands and thousands of years who have walked through worrisome times. I put myself in the shoes of King Jehoshaphat. He was a leader that led with integrity. Things were going great until "Some people came and told Jehoshaphat, 'A vast army is coming against you from Edom, from the other side of the Dead Sea'" (2 Chronicles 20:2, NIV). Bam. This could have sent him into a whirlwind of fear and anxiety. An army much larger than them. His first reaction could have been to panic. But, it wasn't. Instead, he turned to the Lord.

Alarmed, Jehoshaphat resolved to inquire of the Lord, and he proclaimed a fast for all Judah. The people of Judah came together to seek help from the Lord; indeed, they came from every town in Judah to seek him.

Winning the Wrestle with Worry

Then Jehoshaphat stood up in the assembly of Judah and Jerusalem at the temple of the Lord in the front of the new courtyard and said:

"Lord, the God of our ancestors, are you not the God who is in heaven? You rule over all the kingdoms of the nations. Power and might are in your hand, and no one can withstand you. Our God, did you not drive out the inhabitants of this land before your people Israel and give it forever to the descendants of Abraham your friend? They have lived in it and have built in it a sanctuary for your Name, saying, 'If calamity comes upon us, whether the sword of judgment, or plague or famine, we will stand in your presence before this temple that bears your Name and will cry out to you in our distress, and you will hear us and save us.'
2 Chronicles 20:3-9, NIV

Jehoshaphat knew who was in control. He knew the Lord would hear them and save them. It didn't matter how grim it may have appeared or how many people were in the armies surrounding them, they trusted God would deliver them.

The story continues with a promise from the Lord.

Then the Spirit of the Lord came on Jahaziel son of Zechariah, the son of Benaiah, the son of Jeiel, the son of Mattaniah, a Levite and descendant of Asaph, as he stood in the assembly.

He said: "Listen, King Jehoshaphat and all who live in Judah and Jerusalem! This is what the Lord says to you: 'Do not be afraid or discouraged because of this vast army. For the battle is not yours, but God's. Tomorrow march down against them. They will be climbing up by the Pass of Ziz, and you will find them at the end of the gorge in the Desert of Jeruel. You will not have to fight this battle. Take up your positions; stand firm and see the deliverance the Lord will give you, Judah and Jerusalem. Do not be afraid; do not be discouraged. Go out to face them tomorrow,

Marrying Freedom

and the Lord will be with you.'"

Jehoshaphat bowed down with his face to the ground, and all the people of Judah and Jerusalem fell down in worship before the Lord. Then some Levites from the Kohathites and Korahites stood up and praised the Lord, the God of Israel, with a very loud voice.
2 Chronicles 20:14-19, NIV

What if that was our reaction to news or events that stirred worry inside of us? What if we approached it in confidence instead of cowering? Can we change our habits from speaking words of defeat before we even take a step to approaching fear-invoking moments with worship and praise? What would it look like if you paused, laid your worries at Jesus' feet, and then proceeded?

I'll tell you what it looked like for them!

Early in the morning they left for the Desert of Tekoa. As they set out, Jehoshaphat stood and said, "Listen to me, Judah and people of Jerusalem! Have faith in the Lord your God and you will be upheld; have faith in his prophets and you will be successful. "After consulting the people, Jehoshaphat appointed men to sing to the Lord and to praise him for the splendor of his holiness as they went out at the head of the army, saying:

"Give thanks to the Lord, for his love endures forever."

As they began to sing and praise, the Lord set ambushes against the men of Ammon and Moab and Mount Seir who were invading Judah, and they were defeated. The Ammonites and Moabites rose up against the men from Mount Seir to destroy and annihilate them. After they finished slaughtering the men from Seir, they helped to destroy one another.

When the men of Judah came to the place that overlooks the desert and looked toward the vast army, they saw only

dead bodies lying on the ground; no one had escaped. So Jehoshaphat and his men went to carry off their plunder, and they found among them a great amount of equipment and clothing and also articles of value—more than they could take away. There was so much plunder that it took three days to collect it.
2 Chronicles 20: 20-25, NIV

They approached it in praise and ended with so much plunder, it took them days to collect. They trusted, and the Lord provided: "And the kingdom of Jehoshaphat was at peace, for his God had given him rest on every side" (2 Chronicles 20:30, NIV).

Rest on every side. That's what we can have, too! We are reminded if God is on our side, it will be fine. We don't need to find our comfort in the world around us but in the Word. We can turn to the news which changes every day, sometimes every hour. In the media, it's hard to distinguish between what's true and what's being scripted to evoke deep fear. I don't think we will ever know the full truth. Not on this side of heaven.

We have the ability to make the decision: we can turn to all of the uncertain words of man, or we can turn to the truth in the Word of God, which never changes. No matter how much time passes, His truths are the only things that will EVER remain the same. No matter what we go through, no matter what people claim to be true, what stands in His Word will forever remain.

And so, rather than being bogged down with worry, we can be deeply rooted and live like trees planted beside a stream:

But blessed is the one who trusts in the Lord, whose confidence is in him. They will be like a tree planted by the water that sends out its roots by the stream. It does not fear when heat comes; its leaves are always green. It has no worries in a year of drought and never fails to bear fruit."
Jeremiah 17:7-8, NIV

Marrying Freedom

How do we become like the tree that always has green leaves and bears fruit, when it seems we live in a society that thrives on worry? Don't we live in a time in history where it appears the media is excited with bad, scary circumstances? Drama for reporters means a new, hot topic to headline the segment, an article that can be posted online or shared on the front page of the newspaper. Hot news means fiery ratings, something that will draw viewers back to their station to hear the status of the story. That's not the action we should take if we want to quiet our minds. To become like the tree, we must be intentional with where we put our attention and time.

The news station's ratings might be at their peak when they are sharing stories that will instill deep worry in their viewers' hearts, but God's news for you will cause your worries to plummet. He doesn't come with stories that are fear-provoking. He comes with stories of salvation, faithfulness, victory, and hope. His ratings for coming through are always five-star.

We don't have to believe the lie that there isn't any good in the world, because there certainly is. There is tons of good around us; it's often overlooked and a little less popular to share. We must remember: that which we focus on will expand. If we fill our minds 95% of the time with worrisome news, when we look at the world around us, all we are going to see are things that provoke worry. Flip that switch, friend!

What would happen if we focused our thoughts and noticed the GOOD in the world and the people around us? If we spend 95% of our days full of gratitude, repeating the promises of God from His Word, and soaking up the intricate details in how He has strung everything together, what would happen? Boy, I bet our mindset would shift dramatically.

If you aren't sure which promises will help you with worry, try reflecting on this one:

"Therefore I tell you, do not worry about your life, what you will eat or drink; or about your body, what you will wear. Is

*not life more than food, and the body more than clothes?
Look at the birds of the air; they do not sow or reap or
store away in barns, and yet your heavenly Father feeds
them. Are you not much more valuable than they?*
Matthew 6:25-26, NIV

We don't need to worry about what we will eat or what we
will drink, the details that we need every single day to survive.
Don't you think if He has that covered, He will handle the
biggest issues as well?

Whatever your worries look like, rest today knowing He has
it all under control. We're always under His watchful eye, and
nothing comes as a surprise to Him. We don't need to worry
when we have the King of Glory on our side.

Wherever you go, whatever you do. Whether it's traveling
somewhere new, taking an exam for school, wondering how
you'll pay the bills this month, or thinking about the health
of a loved one—whatever you fret about—when thoughts of
worry start to pop into your head, overpower them with
even more thoughts of power and God's truths:

*Peace I leave with you; my peace I give you. I do not
give to you as the world gives. Do not let your hearts be
troubled and do not be afraid.*
John 14:27, NIV

*Do not let your hearts be troubled. You believe in God;
believe also in me.*
John 14:1, NIV

*Let the peace of Christ rule in your hearts, since as members
of one body you were called to peace. And be thankful.*
Colossians 3:15, NIV

Anxiety weighs down the heart, but a kind word cheers it up.
Proverbs 12:25, NIV

The world will try to sway us every which way, none of which align with His peace. When Jesus died for us, He left us with His peace. It's not what the world gives. It's contrary to what the world news, the hottest online articles, and the neighbors across the street want us to believe. What's here on earth is only here. It's temporary. Like the events that pass each day, they come and go, just as the world's worries come and go.

Rather than blanketing conversations with the broken, let's boost them with beauty. Let's promote more of the good in the world. Choose to be the light. You can light up the dark corners of the world and spread positivity. You might look different and crazy to others, but hey, the spark has to start somewhere, so why not let it start with you?

You can't always change what's happening around you, but there are certain things you can change, and all it takes is one small step. It takes you standing up to those internal demons and saying, "Not today." No more focusing on the negative; today, I choose to see the good. Today, I choose to be the good.

One small action can impact a life, which in turn, can impact another, and before you know it, ten lives are affected. Rather than the town and world around us being flattened with worry, as if struck by a twister, let us flatten the worry and rebuild the town with love, peace, joy, and encouragement.

It could be as simple as a positive note of encouragement to a friend, or even leaving a note on someone's windshield, or buying coffee for a friend. It could be paying for the person behind you in the drive-thru, smiling at a stranger you pass, or asking to pray for someone going through a difficult time. Maybe it's listening to someone who needs a shoulder to lean on. Fast from negative speaking. If you notice every word you speak is about all of the bad things taking place, see how long you can go without having conversations about those topics. If you slip, start over. See if you can go a whole week without speaking anything negative; then, keep building from there. Big or small, you can and will make an impact.

Don't let worry become the backseat driver trying to make you turn left when you're supposed to be turning right, stopping you when you're supposed to be accelerating, or causing you to yield when you're supposed to be going. You have the top driver in the universe directing your route. He has everything mapped out. He knows every shortcut, every redirection, every rest stop, and every gas fill-up you'll need. He knows where you will be sidetracked and taken off the main route. He knows when you will need a break. He knows when and how you will be drawn back to Him. He will be there with wide, welcoming arms. He's got all the licenses and credentials, anything and everything you'll ever need to travel along this path He has for you.

He is greater and more powerful. Jesus rose from the dead and performed miracles. God created the entire universe. He's holding everything in His hands. He knows what's coming, and He knows that no matter what it is, He is greater than any struggle, anything that *could* happen, and anything that *will* happen. He's in it, and He's here. He's our seat belt and buckle; He'll protect us from the bumpy ride. He'll be the acceleration we need to outrun the tornado. We won't be destroyed any longer by worry. Instead, we'll accelerate farther from those things that once tried to wipe us out, keeping our eyes ahead on the blue skies of peace and deliverance.

Uncap the Pen:

Is there something you often find yourself worrying about? Is this something logical, or are these scenarios created in your head because of the influences of the world?

____

____

____

Have you noticed a pattern or a trigger that leads to these thoughts? Is it after watching the news, talking to a friend, or some other external factor? What can you do to limit this from happening?

____

____

____

When your mind begins to wander to those things that cause you the deepest worry, choose not to let your mind go there. It has to be a conscious effort. Let the Lord guide you and be your strength. What promises will you focus on next time you feel yourself becoming overwhelmed with worry?

____

____

____

There will always be something bad we can focus on, sometimes to the extent that it makes us forget the good. List a few of the best things that have happened to you this week. When times seem hopeless, reflect on these, and remember His faithfulness through every season.

____

____

____

Sign the Divorce Papers:

"God, you are a God of great power and might. It seems each day the world becomes a darker, scarier place. Help me not to dwell on what's going on around me. Fill my mind with promises of peace. Help me stay focused on the light

You provide. Let no words of doubt or worry come out of my lips. May each word I speak be uplifting and encouraging to those around me. Help me radiate Your light and share Your hope with others. All it takes is one person being light to create a spark that will light a fire in the world around us. Let me be the light. Let me shine for You through every moment of the day. If there are others around me who live in great worry, use me to break through to them. Use me to help them understand who You are to us, so they, too, can live in Your freedom. Thank You for Your great plan and for being bigger than any worry we will ever ponder."

Conditioning for Commitment

This time will be different. I'm ready to commit.

Then, a few months pass.

Are you still on fire, like you were on day one, to the commitment you made? How often do you fulfill it and remain dedicated to it, even when it gets tough, boring, or doesn't turn out as you anticipated?

One of the examples we can probably all relate to is being committed or hearing someone else commit to a gym membership, physical activity, or some sort of healthy living. I worked at a gym for a year, and the membership on January 1 looks a whole lot different than it does on April 15. At the beginning of the year, people decide it's a fresh start. When the clock strikes midnight, they decide this will be the year they will remain committed to a workout routine.

But then . . .
The work schedule fills up.
The kids get busy.
Teachers start handing out tons of homework.
Friends want to go out to dinner.
It gets cold out, so you want to stay in bed, where it's warm, and slowly wake up to have your coffee.

Feelings begin to shift from being on fire for a healthier lifestyle to forfeiting the healthier choices and options. It's so much easier to come up with excuses than it is to drum up excitement, especially when seasons get tough or you lack the desire or energy to fulfill the promise you made to yourself.

Marrying Freedom

No matter what you decide to commit to, it is inevitable. Your feelings and motivations will fade. It's at that moment you can choose to throw in the towel or decide to transform your thinking. You decide to condition yourself and come out stronger. Instead of giving up, you promise yourself you'll give it the one thing you know it needs, *commitment*.

Being committed doesn't limit itself to physical activity or healthy living. It goes much deeper than that. It encompasses many areas of our lives: work, school, convictions, family members. The list goes on.

I've had my fair share of contract jobs after college where I bounced around and worked different events. I was with the same company but experienced different offices, people, and cities. Since I finished that role, I've worked as a substitute teacher, at a country club, a boutique, and a fitness center. I was a recruiter, and now, I work for a marketing firm. I've written articles and blogs for different websites over the years. Cumulatively, it adds up to over six different companies within a seven-year period, and that's not something I'm ashamed of.

In many conversations, especially amongst peers under thirty, people are always talking about keeping their options open. They plan to stay on top of their game, so if a new, flashy opportunity arises, they can jump on it. If they have one bad day at work, they're always keen to explore other options.

In recent months, we've heard headlines of the "Great Resignation." People are switching jobs because better pay and benefits are being offered elsewhere. Employers are desperate for workers, so they're offering sign-on bonuses around every corner. Turnover is high, and people are leaving their place of employment without a second thought, especially if a competitor can offer someone something better. It doesn't matter if they've been there for a year or if it's been twenty years. People crave change, promotion, more money, and better perks. If where they are isn't meeting their expectations or satisfying their needs, it's likely they will be on to the next opportunity.

If a colleague is requiring too much work, or perhaps the project is more challenging than anticipated and the team you work with isn't as fun as your last job, the thoughts begin, *You should start looking for a different job. This isn't the one for you.*

In some cases, it might truly be the wrong fit. But, oftentimes, we see people fleeing at the first moment of discomfort, challenge, boredom, or better opportunity.

We can take it even further than activity and work, and expand upon our commitment to our relationships. How often do we hear people talking about staying in a committed relationship these days? When was the last time I honestly heard someone say something remotely close to that? At a wedding, maybe. In a normal conversation with someone in passing? Very rarely.

What's instead become the norm and topic out of everyone's mouth is this couple is getting divorced. That person is cheating on his/her spouse. Many conversations I've heard have not been a marriage ending due to abuse or unfaithfulness but simply because "it's just not working out anymore. We don't have the feeling we used to, so we're calling it quits." Scarce are the couples who are married for over fifty years. Rare are couples who date for over fifty months, even fifty days.

We hear of couples going through a rough patch. They've both been busy and haven't been paying as much attention to each other or spending quality time together as they used to. When the attractive coworker starts to flirt, they justify it in their heads. It's harmless. It'd never turn into anything. They like the extra attention, the quirky remarks, the back-and-forth banter on work's instant messenger, so they keep it going, back and forth, for months. Eventually, at an after-work gathering, one too many drinks results in them slipping outside together.

One thing leads to another, and before they realize it, they've said and done things they can't take back.

Other times, it's not due to another person. A couples' relationship has been rocky, and it all comes to a head one day when they don't see eye to eye on something. Rather than working things out, they use it as an excuse; it was the end-all, be-all. It was the crutch they needed to lean on, the simplest excuse to give up and sign divorce papers.

What have relationships become? Why don't we sit down and talk through things? Where is the effort to come up with a plan, to work through problems, issues, or concerns? Why don't people consider talking to a counselor? Why has it become ridiculous and unheard of to put some effort into a relationship or marriage? For some, that would mean having to *try*, to be vulnerable, to share things that might not be easy to talk about, and that's why it doesn't happen.

In our over-committed generation, we don't mind putting in the extra time at work, but putting a little extra time into building a stronger relationship isn't always a top priority. Shouldn't it be the other way around? Shouldn't we care more about investing in the foundation of our relationships with our loved ones? Instead, we commit ourselves to unnecessary events and trivial things on our to-do lists, to make a good impression on those around us. Sometimes, those commitments push us even further away from those we care most about.

It's as if everything and everyone's individual wants and needs are important; all of them, except the needs of your spouse, your family, and your closest friends—the ones you say matter most.

I have three nieces, and when I hear them talking about boys, it honestly scares me. First, I cannot believe the youngest one is even old enough to talk about dating. Secondly, their views of dating are very different from when I was growing up.

Conditioning for Commitment

My niece and her friend decided to ask my husband and me for dating advice. The friend had been "dating" her boyfriend for a few months, but they never spent time together and barely even talked to one another. She FaceTimed her ex-boyfriend daily, and she called her current boyfriend "not even cute."

"Should I break up with him," she asked us?

Oh, boy. Dear Lord, help me.

The "looks" thing . . . First, dating is not and should never be about looks and how a person appears on the outside. Appearance is nothing more than what you see, and what you see is not always what you get. Someone could be the most attractive human being you've ever laid eyes on, but they could have the ugliest, most disrespectful, abusive personality.

Would you still think he or she is attractive? Looks ebb and flow with time. Humans change day by day. We're all going to age, get wrinkles, and have gray hair. What's on the outside is inevitably going to change with time. That's a fact.

What's more important than what you see is the inside, someone's heart. God created each and every one of us uniquely, we are ALL masterpieces, not just the male with a six-pack or the female with toned arms. Everyone is created equal, and each and every human is loved and valuable, regardless of outward appearance. No matter the wrinkles, the extra pounds you'd love to lose, and the way your nose is a little crooked from a fall when you were younger . . . God loves it ALL!

Okay, so we had the "looks" conversation with the girls. Then, a conversation about the ex.

I know the feeling of being in a relationship with a guy that secretly talked to his ex, as you learned about in a previous chapter. I know how a situation like that can diminish trust.

Marrying Freedom

Because of that, it caused me to question my value and worth for far longer than it should have. I told her she definitely needed to reevaluate her situation.

The problem is, our generation doesn't like to be lonely. We crave companionship. If we foresee a relationship ending, we want to have someone lined up, so there is no time to be alone without a significant other. We end one relationship, only to spend time with a new person only days, or in some cases, hours, later. However, sometimes, in order to prepare for the right relationship, to heal and mend, and to get in the right place mentally, we have to commit to going through uncomfortable seasons, and one of those seasons might be loneliness.

Being lonely for a while might not be the most enjoyable experience, but it's unfair to you and your boyfriend/girlfriend to remain in a relationship in which you're not one-hundred-and-ten percent committed. By continuing to date this person, you could be missing valuable time that would help you heal and mend your heart, to get you prepared for who or what God is leading you to.

When I stayed in that dysfunctional relationship, it ended badly. It took me a few months to finally cut the cord, and when I did, it still took me a few more months not to be angry, not to let it affect how I viewed myself. The longer I stayed in it, the more damage I did, and in turn, the more time it took me to be okay again.

I didn't date anyone for three years after that, though there were a couple of guys I "talked" to. I was highly cautious of bringing up the "dating" word because I knew that none of them would dare commit to an actual relationship. I felt as if I was walking on pins and needles, dancing around the topic, because I knew it wouldn't turn out the way I was hoping.

If you're thinking I should have walked away then, you are right. Nevertheless, I did not, and hence, why I can stand as the perfect example of why it's wise not to put yourself in a similar situation.

Conditioning for Commitment

If they can't commit to being exclusive with you, and it's something you're longing for, don't throw a fit; just know it probably isn't the right person for you. It won't end well. He or she probably isn't going to fall for you because you give them space. Giving them space is likely going to encourage them to become sly and more noncommittal. You give them an inch, and they'll likely take a foot in the opposite direction with someone else.

One guy I communicated with in that three-year period let me know, from the start, "he wouldn't be ready to date me any time soon" because he "just got out of a relationship," but he still "liked me so much." It didn't make sense to me, but he wanted to spend as much time together as our schedules allowed, so I figured he would be ready sooner or later. I was okay with the lack of commitment. What I should have said was, "See ya!" Instead, I quickly developed feelings, spent time with him daily, and pictured my future with no one but him. It didn't happen, and he soon moved on. Though we were never officially in a "relationship", it was definitely the most painful heartbreak I have experienced. Hey, I know . . . I did it to myself!

Ladies, gentlemen, whoever is reading this, don't settle for lack of commitment in your life. Don't crave companionship from others just to fill your loneliness. Choose to find contentment in God's current path for you while you wait for the right person.

In the meantime, do the things you love to do. Pursue activities that bring you joy. Don't turn on your phone and scroll through the feeds, liking cute photos, hoping, just maybe, they'll see you like it and strike up a conversation.

When my husband started pursuing me, he was intentional. He always made sure I knew where he stood and how he felt about me. He didn't prance around the topic; he was all about it. He didn't wait until the weekend to see if other events came up; he planned to spend time with me, and not hours in advance but days in advance. He didn't want to wait; he wanted to ask me to be his girlfriend and not put it off any longer.

I didn't even know guys these days asked girls to be their girlfriends, and there he was, doing just that. We hung out for close to two months before he even held my hand. He paid for my meals and coffee before we were "dating." We're almost a year into marriage now, and he continues to remind me every single day how much he cares for me. Yes, I know, it's hard to believe, but there are still good people out there!

The funny and ridiculous thing is, sometimes, it is hard for me to accept this. There has been more than one occasion in which my past has affected how I react to this kind of love. There are days I don't feel like I deserve something and someone so sweet. There are days when my self-sufficiency causes me not to be as open in communication as I should be, and it causes him to feel as if I don't trust him. There are days when we get on each other's nerves. There are times when our schedules are so busy, we barely talk for two minutes, and we feel distant from one another. There have been challenges we've had to face and walk through, but what is the one thing that has made all of the difference, through every good and challenging moment? Commitment.

Remember the girls I talked about earlier? What did my niece's friend have in her life? Commitment. Though it was misplaced at the time, and outside of her relationship, it was there. She knew, when she sought advice about her predicament, something wasn't right. Things felt off in her relationship because she was still in conversation with someone she cared about and wanted in her life. Not long after we chatted, she ended things with her boyfriend. That was a few years ago. If we fast forward to now, how do you think things played out? Just as we anticipated they would. She is back with the one she FaceTimed daily. They've been together for quite some time now. Though there have been challenging times as they've grown together through the awkward teen years, they've worked through each season. The thing they aren't lacking? Commitment.

Conditioning for Commitment

Though in this example, the couple did end up together, that's not how it will play out for all. For some, God's plan might not involve a significant other. He created some of us to never marry. A lot of us would freak out at the thought of being single forever, but honestly, being single has gotten a bad rep. Just because one is single doesn't mean that person doesn't have a purpose and therefore should live every single day with a sulky and disappointing outlook.

How about shifting your perspective? Have you ever thought that living single can mean living with impact? Sure, you might not be coming home to a spouse every night, but that gives you ample opportunity to spend time pouring into and loving on those you come into contact with, and to pour into yourself. If you're single, know your fervent love for others makes the Devil's bones jingle. He's shaking in his boots because of the difference you're making.

You might not be married, but God's plan is married to you, and He's going to use your life to birth revival, redemption, peace, and purpose. Are you ready for it? What could that look like? Keep an eye out, because there will be levels of commitment required for many different aspects of your life.

Regardless if it's a big or small commitment, it will take a total surrender. It requires you to keep the promise you made to yourself, no matter how you are feeling, even on days when you're exhausted, busy, and frustrated. Even then, you'll have to put forth the effort to keep pushing through. This commitment won't come without costs. It won't be easy breezy. There will be days you want to make excuses, just as in the parable of the Great Banquet.

A certain man was preparing a great banquet and invited many guests. At the time of the banquet he sent his servant to tell those who had been invited, 'Come, for everything is now ready.'

"But they all alike began to make excuses. The first said, 'I have just bought a field, and I must go and see it. Please

excuse me.'
"Another said, 'I have just bought five yoke of oxen, and I'm
on my way to try them out. Please excuse me.'
"Still another said, 'I just got married, so I can't come.'

"The servant came back and reported this to his master.
Then the owner of the house became angry and ordered
his servant, 'Go out quickly into the streets and alleys of
the town and bring in the poor, the crippled, the blind and
the lame.'

"'Sir,' the servant said, 'what you ordered has been done,
but there is still room.'

"Then the master told his servant, 'Go out to the roads
and country lanes and compel them to come in, so that
my house will be full. I tell you, not one of those who were
invited will get a taste of my banquet.'"
Luke 14:16-24, NIV

Which person will you be? The one making excuses or the one who chooses to sit down, enjoy the feast and the abundance God has for you?

Whether you're single, dating, engaged, or married, you get to decide. Only you can decide whether you'll be casual with your commitments or if you'll work with intentionality and dedication.

Many times, it starts with a promise to yourself. Will you pursue the path that develops a better version of yourself and stick with it?

Have you incorporated daily routines? Do you remain committed to them? Morning and evening routines can be life-changing. Have you considered starting one, if you haven't already? They can help you move with purpose. If you miss your routine one day, don't get frustrated. Don't beat yourself up over it. Just pick back up where you left off, and don't miss one day, two days in a row.

Conditioning for Commitment

What about your family members? Are you committed to your relationships with them? Do they see you and talk to you on a regular basis, or are you so committed to your work or other obligations that time passes without seeing or connecting with them?

How are your friendships? Have you taken a few moments recently to send a text to your friend or even given them a call to check in and see how they are doing?

Are you taking care of yourself- physically, emotionally, and spiritually? Do you devote time to exercise, quiet time, and things that fill your cup?

Are you committed, or are you cowering from the things that could build a better you to carry out the things you were created to do?

When you decide to do something, to be something, to pursue this, or build your skills in that, there are going to be challenges. There are going to be times the Enemy slips thoughts into your head, that it's too hard, that your colleague deserves the promotion, you're not good enough, you don't deserve something so good, or there's better out there.

Don't listen! He is going to try to speak through as many people as possible, and he's going to try to make himself so evident as often as he can. He'll do whatever it takes to make sure you don't keep your commitment.

Next time you have to choose between staying committed or letting the commitment slide, lean into the Lord, draw strength from Him and seek His counsel. He didn't create you to give up on things when they get tough. It's often in the toughest seasons that He does the most beautiful work. Commit to it, and be too obsessed with His plan to quit.

Uncap the Pen:

Think of a time when you committed to something, but the commitment didn't last long. What was it?

____

____

____

Why did your commitment fall through? What made you change your mind? What thoughts did you have that convinced you you didn't need to follow through?

____

____

____

Is this commitment something you truly wanted and still want to this day? If not, what changed?

____

____

____

Next time you're in a similar situation, and you're ready to give up on something you truly want, write a prayer that you can repeat to yourself, to remind yourself why you started and how important it is to give it your all.

____

____

____

____

<u>Sign the Divorce Papers:</u>

"Dear God, I thank You for being the most committed person in my life. No matter how much I mess up, how happy or sad, or how big or small I feel, Your love for me never wavers. In this generation of being committed to many things, we struggle to be committed to what truly matters. Lord, I pray You would give me the endurance to run the race You have set before me. I pray You give me the strength to persevere when it gets tough. I pray to be an example of Your power that shows others it is possible to commit and not quit. You are so much bigger and stronger than the trials and tribulations we face. I want to finish the race You have started me on. When feelings start to fade and defeat and discouragement creep in, I want to give it my all. Thank You, Lord, for showing us the perfect example of this. May I reflect You more and more each day."

Uncovering the Unforgiveness

*Even if they sin against you seven times in a day and seven
times come back to you saying 'I repent,'
you must forgive them.*
Luke 17:4, NIV

I'm sorry; will you please forgive me?

Has someone ever murmured those words to you?

Maybe it was something small, easy to forgive. A tiny mistake.
A slip in judgment. It happens. We were born into a fallen
world, so we're all undoubtedly going to mess up, probably
more than once a day. They aren't always huge mess-ups.

Those kinds of instances are typically pretty easy to sweep
under the rug and forget. We forgive, we learn a lesson, then
we forget the hurt, sometimes never thinking of it again.

Other times, something happens that's more serious, more
emotional, or more damaging to you or someone you care
about. It caused you or that person seemingly unbearable
pain. Maybe it was hurt so deep you didn't want to forgive,
and you don't see how anyone else could either. Perhaps
you want to forgive someday, but for right now, you just want
to stay mad and dwell on it a little bit longer.

Don't we all go through things that cause us to feel this way?
We say we forgive this person but still harbor the mistake.
We hold the grudge and the emotions that came with it,
deep down within us.

*The parent who walked out when you were a child.
The teacher who told you you'd never amount to anything.
The bully who made you insecure and hateful towards
yourself.
The boyfriend who abused you.*

Marrying Freedom

The colleague who took all of the credit for your idea, which got him/her a promotion.
The child who left home and never returned.
The girlfriend who treated you like dirt.
The parent who had an affair, tearing your family apart.
The spouse who walked out when you hit a rough patch.
The friend who stabbed you in the back.

It might continue to eat at you, day in and day out. You don't foresee ever forgiving this person for what he or she did to you. You might have said it was fine and dandy, and you can put on a poker face better than anyone you know, but internally, there's a hurt you can't erase.

Where do you stand on this? Is there something that has happened to you, or someone who has caused you pain, that you can't seem to shake? No matter how much time goes by, does it seem there is nothing that can erase or even ease that memory from your mind?

Well, prepare yourself to resurrect it from the deepest chambers of your heart. It's time to face those situations, those people, and those things that hurt you. Maybe not face-to-face, but together with Jesus. He's here to help you break free from those heavy chains and give you freedom like never before. It won't be easy. It's probably going to take some humility and strength to do it, but we're in this together.

If we're being real and transparent with one another, I think we can all agree each of us has been hurt by someone in our life, in one way or another. We have demons we battle. We are each upset, angered, challenged, and saddened by different things. What causes harm to one will do absolutely nothing to another. We're all different, which can make forgiveness a tricky subject, especially if someone doesn't even realize they have hurt you.

Can you picture in your mind, right now, someone you had a disagreement with, a falling out with, or a fight with? Did someone abandon you at some point, or have you had a misunderstanding of some sort? Does this person know he or she caused you harm or hurt, or have you just assumed that they should realize? To you, it seemed obvious this person should know they caused you pain. However, that isn't always the case.

Whatever this looks like for you, if you are seeking vengeance for what was done to you, try this instead: "Keep your tongue from evil and your lips from telling lies. Turn from evil and do good; seek peace and pursue it" (Psalm 34:13-14, NIV).

You might want to rattle off some strong words to this person, to make them hurt like you are hurting. I am right there with you. I've had to bite my tongue more times than I'd like to admit. There have even been times when I haven't, but we must try. We must show the love of Jesus and be the bigger person.

If you come across the person that has hurt you, rather than making a war scene, make it a scene for prayer. You can pray absolutely anywhere, and it can be your greatest weapon in battle. You don't even have to say hello. Just turn and walk the other way and say a prayer under your breath for them.

They might have hurt you, but don't let the hurt deter you. The Lord wants you to turn away from evil, and do what is good. Let prayer be your sword, rather than words that sting or actions to hurt. The weapon of prayer is so much sharper than anything else in this world. You might not want to take out that piece of equipment because you'd rather do anything else but say a prayer for them. Still, you can find hope and reassurance in remembering that, "Though they plot evil against you and devise wicked schemes, they cannot succeed" (Psalm 21:11, NIV).

Have I struggled with this? Have I wanted to approach the person, causing embarrassment and pain, and tell them to snap out of their wicked ways? Absolutely. It's still something I struggle with and am working through to this day. There is one person, in particular, that always seems to get my blood boiling. If I see them, I know I instantly have to start praying, because I need the Lord to guide my tongue and heart. It's someone who has caused me so much pain, it's hard to forget. It didn't stop with me, but further when they did and said things to people I care about that also caused them pain. One mention of their name can instantly get my blood pressure up because I know, whenever it's mentioned, it's never because of a happy situation. It's always a story of deception, deceit, and manipulation. I know that's not a great example for you because I am still walking through it myself. But that's life. I'm not going to pretend like I have every topic in this book figured out, because I don't! I am aware of my weaknesses, and I am working through them.

The funny thing is, for so long, I honestly thought I had forgiven this person. I thought I was over it and everything they had done, when, indeed, it was quite the opposite.

Though I never received an apology for things that had been done to me, I thought I could look past that fact. Let's just say *thought* is the huge keyword. I decided I would simply acknowledge what was done, feel the emotions from it, and let it go, never to bother me again.

However, the time came when I realized, instead of forgiving and forgetting, I had been festering. I became an expert at mentally blocking out thoughts of this person, who was at the root of the pain. I had "forgiven" them in my eyes. I never saw them, and they didn't have any part in my life, so why should I allow someone I never associated with to slip chains of bitterness around my ankles and wrists?

You would think, "Out of sight, out of mind" right? Well, that's what I was pretty sure I had achieved. Why would I unknowingly sit on any negative emotions for so long? I didn't think I had. A recent sermon given at church about forgiving others spurred some unexpected emotions. The pastor asked us to close our eyes and walked us through a step-by-step process, allowing us to uncover any unforgiveness we had harbored in our hearts.

In the end, I asked myself: Am *I honestly in a state where I could agree, wholeheartedly, that I had forgiven?* Judging by the tears I couldn't stop from streaming down my face, I'd say evidently not.

Not long after that sermon, I saw this person, smiling, acting as if nothing had happened.

Okay, this will be fine. I smiled and waved, but as I sat there, my hands began to shake, my feet began to tap on the floor, and all of the words I wanted to say boiled inside. *Lord Jesus, give me strength. I know You're in control. I know You do not need me to say or do anything, but simply smile and say hello.*

Well, so much for letting the past slide . . . Now what?

How had I been so certain I'd let it all go, when in fact, I'd only locked it deep under the surface? I'd pushed it into the closet, turned the key, and made sure it was triple-bolted so that not even the slightest crack of light could get through. It was still there, just deeply and very well hidden. I was compartmentalizing and doing the finest job. I was covering it up and not working through my emotions, which, in turn, only escalated the emotions I felt when I saw this person. I definitely hadn't forgiven like I thought I had.

From that day forward began the process of unveiling those situations, the people and the things that had deeply hurt me in the past. It takes surrendering each and every day. It's asking God to reveal those places, to find peace with them.

For some issues, there isn't a clear answer as to why things turned out the way they did, and that's the hardest part. It's not understanding, not knowing the full story, not really having a reason to explain why things are the way they are, but still having to come to peace with them.

If you're like me, you like to understand. I like to have an explanation, a detailed summary of things. When that isn't given, I want to uncover the reason, do research, and find a formula that will allow me to make it all make sense. However, God doesn't always show us or tell us why something is happening the way it is. Instead, He teaches us to trust Him through it. That can be the hardest part: trusting when you're trying to understand, but there's just no clear explanation for it.

Sometimes, it means we will have to cry out to Him in anger, frustration, impatience, disappointment, pain, and confusion. Sometimes, we will be at a loss for words, so we won't even be able to tell Him how we're feeling. There will be times we will just sit and not say or think a thing, but the Lord will know each and every time how we're feeling and the exact emotions we want to express but cannot muster up.

I've been there. I've sat with tears streaming down my face and told the Lord, "God, I don't even know what to say right now. I know you know what I'm feeling. Search my heart, and be the things you know I need right now." It's hard to put those needs into words, but the amazing thing is, we don't have to. We don't have to spell out exactly what it is when we can't describe it. Our good Father knows.

When He knows our needs and cries of our heart, but we can't put anything into words, it takes a lot of trust, a lot of what feels like taking step after step, with a blindfold over our eyes. Our eyes might be covered, but He still sees all. The view might be fuzzy in front of us, but His is a picture-perfect polaroid of deliverance.

We have to remember that what we see and what we experience is only a small frame in the window of life. It's only a fraction of eternity. Some things won't make sense on this side of heaven. Other things will make sense, and we'll realize the good that came from them.

Sometimes the uncertainty and pain seem too big, too real, too fresh, and too raw. There are times we want to just sit in it, to soak in it like a hot bubble bath after a long day. We want the bubbles to flow over the tub, cover us, and stay in that spot, soaking in the emotions that the person or situation brought on.

It's okay to do that. It's good, even smart, to experience those emotions, to walk through them, and to let them run their course in you. However, you don't have to be a straight-A student to know that it's not smart to stay there.

All hot bubble baths eventually turn cold. Your skin will start to wrinkle up. Your bubbles will disappear. Just as there's only a certain length of time the bath will be that perfect temperature to soak in, there is a length of time for you to remain stricken by the emotion of your situation.

Don't let it take up too much of your tomorrow. Get up, and get out of it. Dry yourself off, and leave it feeling refreshed, ready to conquer your giants. Don't let the situation conquer you. Don't bathe in the waters of bitterness. You are made for more than holding a grudge and letting it consume you and your days.

Rather than staying there, pray through it. It might make no sense to you, and maybe you've never said a single prayer in your life, but hear me out. Pray for them. Pray for those people, that individual, that situation that's caused you pain, that you can't seem to shake.

That's what I started to do. Every time I passed the house of a person who hurt me, instead of becoming sad as I drove by, I would pray for that person. I prayed (and still pray) that they know how deeply they are loved. I pray for peace, I pray for fulfillment, and I pray for goodness and fruitfulness over the situation.

It might not make sense, and you might not want to do it, but just start and try it out. If you have ever read or heard of the story of David and Saul in 1 Samuel, you see how doing this can play out. Saul knew the Lord had chosen David to one day become king, even though Saul's son should have technically taken the throne after Saul died. Saul tried everything in his power to make sure that didn't happen.

David was on the run most of his life because Saul continuously plotted evil against him. Saul even tried multiple times to end David's life. One would think David would rejoice when the day finally came that Saul passed, but what did David do?

Then David and all the men with him took hold of their clothes and tore them. They mourned and wept and fasted till evening for Saul and his son Jonathan, and for the army of the Lord and for the nation of Israel, because they had fallen by the sword.
2 Samuel 1:11-12, NIV

He celebrated the life and legacy of Saul. Saul never stopped attempting to destroy David, yet David chose to honor Saul's life.

Wow. Can you imagine yourself forgiving someone who tried to kill you multiple times? For me, that'd be a huge challenge! However, seeing God's faithfulness throughout David's story shows that it can be done. We have the power to choose. We can choose to let the situations we go through make us bitter or allow them to change us and make us better.

Like David, who could have easily lived a bitter, angry life, we, too, can seek God's direction and guidance and allow Him to fill us up, as He did in this story. Let's choose to be better than the enemy. Let's pray it out, and give all our emotions to Christ. Let Him work through the situation. It's the last thing you want to do, I know. I can say that, because I'll tell you one thing, I didn't want to do it either. Once I started, I watched and realized the Lord was indeed doing work on my heart.

You might not ever come to terms with the person you've had on your mind in this chapter, but beauty can still bloom from your story. God doesn't want your heart to be moldy and overtaken by the bad; He wants to mold you and shape your future with His hands. Let your story be one of redemption.

I've come to learn and accept the fulfillment and peace I need are not found in other humans. I don't experience it only when everything is "spic and span," with no problems or disagreements, or when every relationship and situation makes sense. It's here and available to me every moment of the day, just as it is for you.

Give yourself permission to forgive without ever receiving an apology. Chances are, you might never get one. You have to allow yourself to forgive and move on. Grow. Lean into the lessons learned and realize the situation made you into the person you are today, and that it is for a purpose that maybe only God knows.

Turn to a trusted friend or mentor if you need to. Talk with a counselor. Set up a time to meet with the person you've had on your mind. Cry out to God. Share every single emotion you are feeling from whatever caused you pain. Give those emotions over to Him. Saying them out loud or writing them down in your journal can bring such a sense of relief. Don't keep it bottled up any longer. Bless, and release it.

People will say and do things that hurt us, even scar us, changing our lives forever. In those moments, we can choose to harden our hearts, or we can choose to hear Him out. In the most beautiful way, He fills my heart and my life. Allow Him to pour into the spaces in your heart: the ones that were hurt so deeply, that feel so broken, and are filled with bitterness. Let Him seep in with waters so fresh, so clear, so filling, you'd think you stepped into a crystal clear hot spring bath that never turns cold-a bath that doesn't run out of bubbles, that leaves you refreshed, at peace, clean, and whole.

Uncap the Pen:

Are there people or situations in your life that have caused you to be in a state of unforgiveness? Has someone or something hurt you so badly, you don't ever foresee forgiving that individual? Create a list below of things that are taking up space in your heart.

____

____

____

Are these recent happenings or are some of them things that have occupied your mind for longer than you'd like to admit? If you've tried to block them out and keep them hidden, what is it about the situation that seems to keep you hanging on?

____

____

____

Release these situations to the Lord. For each person or thing on your list, say the sentence below, even if you don't believe it; even if you don't want to believe it; even if you have no desire to pray. Release each and every situation over to the Lord. Continue to pray this, day after day, and see what the Lord does in your heart.

"Lord, I release _____________________________ to you."

Write out a prayer below for the things you are going to work through, work on, and let go, so you can find peace and freedom in Christ. Pray this prayer daily. Pray it multiple times per day. Pray it when you have no desire to pray. Just keep praying. Put it somewhere that's easy for you to come back to. Let Christ renew you, your heart, and your outlook, and bring you the peace that only He can give.

____

____

____

____

____

____

<u>Sign the Divorce Papers:</u>

_"Lord, forgiveness is hard. Sometimes, I just want to sit and dwell on the pain that someone has caused me. Sometimes, I want to speak up and pierce their hearts with my words like they once did to me. I don't want to let ______ off the hook; I want to hold this grudge and bitterness against them for just a little while longer. I release it all to You. I know these thoughts don't come from You. I know these emotions are not what You want me to feel towards this person or situation. God, I need you. I need Your peace to fill the devastated places in my heart. I need Your power to mend my heart from the inside out. I thank You for the grace that You show us every single day, and how abundant it is. I pray I show the same grace to those in my life that have caused me or someone I care about harm. I pray Your love would overwhelm those negative feelings and we would all come out of this stronger. I thank You for being the perfect example of forgiveness and pray that, each and every day, I will develop just a little bit more grace than the day before."_

Marrying Freedom

Living After a Loss

The Lord is close to the brokenhearted and saves those
who are crushed in spirit.
Psalm 34:18, NIV

One inevitable part of life is loss. Whether it be the loss of a job, a loved one, a relationship, or your home and personal belongings, we all go through a season of it, eventually. It can be trivial or heart-wrenching.

From the moment we are born, we are continually closer to the day we are going to leave this earth. It's a part of life none of us can escape. We are born, and one day, we will die. Losing someone dear to us is a part of life that will always happen, as much as we wish it wouldn't.

Depending on your connection or attachment to the loss, you may have a terribly tough time walking through it. There are losses that affect every aspect of life, consuming you, and you can't seem to shake the pain.

I sat on the couch, in a shared study room, on the fourth floor of my dorm during my junior year of college. The call came that Jerry had passed away. The man I'd looked up to as a grandfather figure, who had instilled more confidence in me than anyone I'd ever met, gave the best hugs, and was overall one of my favorite people, was gone.

I didn't even know he was sick, let alone in the hospital! How could this be? How was this happening? I didn't even get the chance to say goodbye!

In the days that followed, I felt as if I constantly had a rock in the pit of my stomach. I could barely stand the thought of food, and it was a challenge to hold myself together for my classes and the requirements of my daily schedule. My favorite place became the shower so I could cry my eyes out and no one would know I was crying.

I had never had anyone close to me pass away prior to that, and I certainly didn't want to know how it felt. But there I was. The time came for the funeral and calling hours, and boy was I a mess. It was comforting to be around his family, but it didn't feel the same without him there. I didn't want to know this new normal.

The thoughts were all-consuming for a couple of weeks. Sleep was tough, at first. I just couldn't wrap my head around the fact that he was truly gone. This whole death thing . . . I wasn't a fan. However, I would have to become even more "comfortable" with it, just a month later.

It was a Friday morning, about ten minutes before my 8 a.m. class. I checked my phone before leaving my dorm room and saw I had three missed calls. I know if I ever receive a phone call in the morning, it's typically not for a good reason. Something is usually wrong.

I was standing, looking out the window, when my sister answered her phone, hysterically crying. My thoughts rushed immediately to my grandpa. She's the executor of his will, and since I had missed calls from her and my mom, it had to be him.

"Ryan," she said. "He's gone."

I met Ryan a few years back. He had grown up playing hockey with my nephew. My family and I ventured to a handful of their travel games over the years, where I had become close to a few of my nephew's teammates, Ryan being one of them. He had the absolute kindest heart, was always full of encouragement, and was wise beyond his years. We quickly became good friends and shared lots of heart-to-heart and long conversations.

He planned to go into the Army when he got out of high school. We always joked that once he was there, we'd write letters to each other while he was gone as they did in the movie *Dear John*. Then, we'd eventually get married and live happily ever after.

Now, even joking about that wouldn't be possible. I had just talked to him a week before. How was it possible I wouldn't be able to, ever again?

It's the absolute weirdest feeling trying to wrap your mind around and understand something as final as death, and his passing is one I'll never understand on this side of heaven. He passed away in his sleep at the young and ripe age of seventeen. He had his senior pictures taken but would never have the chance to graduate from high school. *Why, God?*

He was so strong in his faith for his young age, and that was something that struck me vividly. It was a stark contrast to the guys my age and a detail that increased my admiration and respect for him.

How could I pick up my feet and move on when, within weeks, two men that had meant so much to me, both who loved Jesus and instilled so much hope, confidence, and encouragement into my life and helped shape me into the person I am today, were gone?

No more uplifting conversations. No more joking around. No more encouragement. No more hugs. No more "I love yous." Nothing more.

Their deaths were the first time I had to walk through someone close to me passing, and that was tough. I knew they were both with Jesus, free of pain, suffering, and the bad in this world. I knew they were much better off, looking down over all of us, but that certainly didn't make the realization of them being gone any easier.

There were two very logical options I could have taken during this time.

I could have become mad at God and turned away from Him. I didn't understand how He could take either of them, especially so unexpectedly. They were both such incredible people. How was it fair that He decided it was their time?

Marrying Freedom

Why didn't we get a heads up or some sort of sign, so we could at least cherish one more conversation, hug, and I love you? I didn't want to accept it. I didn't want it to be real. I could have turned away right then and there, believing God wouldn't do something like this. He wouldn't take someone from this world that loved Him so much. These were two amazing men. Why them? If God loved us, then He wouldn't allow something like this to happen. I could have decided I didn't need to turn to Him with anything anymore. I could have cut Him out.

Or, I could find comfort in Christ and allow Him to give my weary heart and soul peace in the darkest of nights. I could cry out to Him when I couldn't bear the sadness. I could come to terms with what was and find the strength to continue on, knowing He had a plan for it all, even if it didn't make even the slightest bit of sense.

Thankfully, I chose the latter and allowed this season to be one in which I dug my roots deeper into Christ, deeper than they'd ever gone before. The previous year, I had started regularly attending a Thursday night worship service and Bible study held on my college campus. Through that, I had come to know a whole new side of Jesus than what I'd been taught and known growing up.

God was no longer just in the church, and the church was no longer just something I *had* to do. He was all around, ready to have a conversation at any time of day. He was available in the best of times and at the worst of times. Now, I knew this. My faith would get me through this. I wouldn't allow it to put a damper on my new passion and excitement for living for Christ.

When Lazarus died in John 11, Mary and Martha could have let it destroy them. They could have become bitter and angry towards Jesus for not being there. Their brother was gone, and they knew that if Jesus had been there, Lazarus would likely be alive.

Living After a Loss

*"On his arrival, Jesus found that Lazarus had already been
in the tomb for four days. Now Bethany was less than
two miles from Jerusalem, and many Jews had come to
Martha and Mary to comfort them in the
loss of their brother."*
John 11:17-19, NIV

His death caused weeping, not just among the sisters, but people had come from the surrounding area to comfort the sisters. What came next is told in the shortest sentence in the Bible, but one of the most powerful . . . two simple words, "Jesus wept" (John 11:35, NIV).

Jesus knows and understands the pain we go through. Though Lazarus' story ends differently, as he was raised from the dead, there was still the moment when Jesus experienced and displayed the heartbreak that comes with loss. He can relate to you and the gut-wrenching feeling you are experiencing.

Knowing Jesus was there and knowing what I was feeling was great, but that didn't mean it was easy for me to accept. However, the Lord showed me His overwhelming peace, comfort, and healing. Whether it be from Him queueing a song on the radio with lyrics I needed to hear, at just the right moment, a rainbow in the sky, a conversation with a friend, a much-needed hug, or revealing the perfect Bible verse to me when flipping open my Bible, He kept showing me He was there. He was listening, and He was not going anywhere.

Ryan's favorite Bible verse reads, "They will fight against you but will not overcome you, for I am with you and will rescue you, declares the Lord" (Jeremiah 1:19, NIV).

I leaned into that verse hard. I knew the Enemy wanted me to turn away from God. He wanted me to get mad at God and forget about His promises of comfort, love, and peace. But, the Lord stayed right there with me, helping me overcome the sadness.

Looking back, that was one of the hardest seasons of my life, but it was also one of the most beautiful. I was full of many different emotions, but never once did they overcome me to the point of no return. The Lord was there, rescuing me from the thoughts that would take me down the wrong path, from the pain that seemed unbearable at times, and from the lack of understanding I felt day after day. Sure, those things were fighting against me, and the Devil tried to use them to take over, but God is so much bigger than any schemes the Enemy comes to play with.

Ryan and Jerry were both strong Christians, and that is something I wanted to continue to build upon and carry to those around me. Like them, I too would be a light to this dark world. I wouldn't let the trials and tribulations this life brings get me down. I would continue to love others, to live a life representative of Jesus. I want to live in a way that when others look at me, they think something is different about me. After learning more, they'd realize that the difference was Jesus living in and shining through me. Through my example, they would learn they could experience the love of Jesus for themselves, too.

Death reminds me of the frailty of this life. The world we live in is so temporary. We have to remember when we face the death of a loved one, a friend, a family member, or even a stranger in the newspaper or on the evening news, it is a part of life.

As death typically does, it occurs when we least expect it, just as Ryan and Jerry's did. We don't foresee it, because we don't want to think about having to live without someone we care about. But when it does happen, we can let it destroy us. We can let the passing of someone we care about take us down a dark path of depression.

Maybe we did not say goodbye. Maybe it was an illness that took someone too soon. Maybe the person was not a believer. We might not know for sure if they believed, and that drives us crazy.

Living After a Loss

The last conversation we had with that person could have been full of arguing and hateful words.

We can replay the moments over and over in our heads, the conversations we would have had, could have had, should have had, but that isn't going to change anything. We can wish we would have said that, wish we would have heard them declare they believed in Jesus, or wish we could take back those words we said to them, but none of those things are going to do us any good.

We can allow regrets or thoughts to consume our daily thoughts, making it nearly impossible to do anything but mourn their loss. Or, we can choose to continue living our lives as that individual would have wanted us to. Celebrate their life and who they were. Talk about them. Create an event in honor of them. Share what we're going through with others. We don't have to go through this alone!

We can honor them and carry on their legacy by living each day to the fullest. Their death can serve as a reminder that we have to keep living because we only have so much time on this earth, and we mustn't waste it. We're here for a purpose, so we must pick up our shoes, slip them back on, and keep walking with intentionality and urgency down the path the Lord has drawn.

It might seem unfair to live and enjoy life after they are gone. But you must. You must pick up your feet and put one foot in front of the other. You must focus on that until you can move, until you can see past the pain their death has caused, until you see the shining promise Christ has never left you and will rescue you in your darkest hour.

It took me a while to put the above words into practice. With each passing day, I worked on shifting my focus from the hurting and wishing things were different, to the precious moments He was blessing me with. I knew I had the power to control what I thought; I was just allowing the sadness to overwhelm me and take over. Finally, I began making more of an effort to control those thoughts, to be aware of when I was falling into the pit of depressed thinking.

If you're like me, it might take everything inside of you to think of the good, to find happiness and appreciation in the midst of the pain. Don't give up on yourself because God hasn't given up on you. Just keep going. The Lord is with you. He will never leave, and though this time is difficult, He is bigger than the pain. He is watching over you and will carry you when you feel as if you can't go on any longer. He'll do it for you, and He'll keep doing it for you, until you can do it for yourself again.

Uncap the Pen:

Have you lost someone you were close to? How did this affect you and your daily life?

____

____

____

If you could have one more conversation with this person, what would you say?

____

____

____

____

What is one thing you learned from this person that you want to carry on as a legacy?

____

____

____

When you start to get down, what is one thing you want to remember from this person that will give you strength, hope, and courage to continue living your life to the fullest?

____

____

____

<u>Sign the Divorce Papers:</u>

"Lord, You know my heart. You know what I am feeling. You know all I have been through, all I have seen and heard. You know how death has impacted and influenced my life. You know the things I would change, the words I would or wouldn't have said, and You see the full scope of it. Lord, I know that death is a part of life, but that doesn't make facing it any easier. Be my strength when I am weak, be my hope when I start to fall, and carry me when I can't take the next step. Lord, thank you for this life. I don't want to remain chained to the what-ifs, the moments that I cannot change. Lord, help me to carry on the legacy, to live a full life for those who, it feels, have gone too soon. I know we're only here for a short time, so help me to live to my fullest potential for You here on this Earth. Thank you for Your strength, Your healing, and Your power. Thank you for loving me, carrying me, for sending little reminders, throughout my day, of the beauty of life, and for being exactly what I need every day. I love You, Lord."

Signing the Papers

The jury is here waiting to declare the verdict. Have you signed all of your papers? Did you uncap your pen and write your signature on the lines, declaring you're divorcing each and every chain, every distraction, every lie and doubt that has been delaying the plans and purpose of your life? It's time to step into the freedom available to you!

Your slate is clean. Your sentence is cleared. You can slip off the chains. You can walk with a pep in your step into the abundance the Lord has for you.

There are so many chains that can hold us back from being what God created us to be. Maybe you're thinking to yourself, *Hilary, you didn't mention the chain that has me tied to the ground and wall so fiercely.*

If you didn't even acknowledge it, how am I supposed to break free of it?
Does this mean that my struggle isn't important or worthy of being talked about?
Great; I read this book thinking I would find freedom, but here I am. It's hopeless.

Sweet reader, if I did not discuss the challenges that are evident in your life, do not count them as any less important. Do not think they don't matter.

After reading through these pages, what is the one thing that has remained a constant in every single story?

In the anxiety, in the comparison, loss, unforgiveness, patience, and worry...

God's faithfulness.

I know, there are heavier chains that have the ability to hold

us captive: Addiction, pornography, pride, guilt, shame, violence, abuse, greed, and regret.
No matter what it is, whether it's covered here or not, you don't have to remain chained down any longer.

The list of chains we have in our lives is exhaustive, but the Lord never tires. He doesn't need a timeout. The same God who was faithful in every circumstance here will be faithful in every battle for you.

The same God who overcame the anxiety will overcome your addiction.
The same God who conquered unforgiveness will cast out your regret.

It doesn't matter what you're walking through or the path that you've been on.

You can rest, assured God will be there every step of the way. When it gets tough, and you want to give up, He will be a steady hand to guide you back to Him.

It probably won't be easy, and the battle won't look the same for everyone, but remember, it's a battle for your mind, and "the mind governed by the flesh is death, but the mind governed by the Spirit is life and peace" (Romans 8:6, NIV).

When your mind is focused on the here and now, the Devil will try to show up in every way possible. He will use every tactic in his playbook to try and sneak in to chain you up again. He'll use your loved ones, best friends, and people at work. He will exhaust every timeout, every halftime meeting, and every second he can get to interfere with God's plan for your life. He knows what triggers you, tempts you, and distracts you, and bet your bottom dollar, he will use it all.

When you set your mind on Christ, on the power that lives inside of you through Him, you will be filled with life and peace. The Devil is getting a technical; he's getting ejected from the game.

Signing the Papers

The playbook looks a lot different once he's gone. You feel love, joy, peace, patience, kindness, goodness, faithfulness, gentleness, and self-control overflowing inside of you.

You notice, as you're leaving the game, the Devil is bound to the wall right outside. He isn't far away, and he'll try to squirm his way back into your life. He'll try to remove the chains from himself and place them back on you. He'll do whatever he can to take you back to the things that once held you captive. He'll try to come back with a vengeance, and he will bring along his friends.

"When an impure spirit comes out of a person, it goes through arid places seeking rest and does not find it. Then it says, 'I will return to the house I left.' When it arrives, it finds the house unoccupied, swept clean and put in order. Then it goes and takes with it seven other spirits more wicked than itself, and they go in and live there. And the final condition of that person is worse than the first. That is how it will be with this wicked generation."
Matthew 12:43-45, NIV

He'll try to make you worse off. Don't look back.

We will have trouble. We will all fall down and fall short. We will all become discouraged, disheartened, and feel like complete failures at times.

Remember how far you've come. Remember God's faithfulness in the past. Trust His plans in the present, and be expectant for His faithfulness in the future. He's not going to let you down.

As I finished up my first twenty-one-day fast, God pressed a thought on my heart. During those twenty-one days, I read food labels more often and much more attentively than in the past. I paid attention to any added sugars or processed ingredients and avoided those. I looked for pure foods—unprocessed, natural.

Marrying Freedom

If you go to the store, the options are overwhelming. There are gluten-free, vegan, and sugar-free options. Food can be packaged and prepared in so many different ways, and all you have to do is look at the labels to see what it contains. The ingredients put together can be changed to create different recipes and outcomes.

The same goes for our hearts. God sees and knows our hearts completely. Each is full of different ingredients: love, peace, joy, clarity, regret, shame, comparison, unrest, addiction, and unforgiveness. These aren't permanent. We have the ability to change what our hearts, bodies, and souls are made of.

When we make the decision to partner with Christ, we will see our lives change. We will feel the shackles loosen, as we take a step toward freedom. As we hand over each distraction, decision, and trial to him, we feel a little stronger. We release the things that held us back. We start to gain momentum. We feel more confident and lighter than we ever have. Remember how heavy your chains were before. You might have thought you'd never be able to take them off, yet here you are, on a journey to walking freely in His grace, mercy, and love.

You feel as light as the air you breathe, and you can't help but smile at the miracle He's done. He changed up the ingredients. He did a work in your heart that changed your entire composition.

You were once dead; now you're alive.

And if the Spirit of him who raised Jesus from the dead is living in you, he who raised Christ from the dead will also give life to your mortal bodies because of his Spirit who lives in you.
Romans 8:11, NIV

The verdict is in. Your chains are gone. You are set free; you feel the relief I felt when I walked out of the police station that Halloween night. Your sentence is cleared. You're free to go. Take a deep breath, and inhale the possibilities before you. You have finalized your divorce. Your papers are signed, sealed, and delivered. You're His! You're married to Jesus' mighty promises of freedom. You've uncapped your potential. It's time to walk into the abundance He has for you. Congratulations!

 Hilary Frank is a wife, mom, daughter, sister, and friend born and raised on a farm in central Illinois. It was there where she fell in love with the beauty of the countryside and spent many hours reading, journaling, writing, and dreaming of making an impact on the world through her words. She received her business degree from Illinois Wesleyan University with a concentration in Marketing.

For over five years, she has been writing content that empowers people to find peace, joy, contentment, and abundance in the day-to-day. She is a contributing writer for Reclaim Today and has been featured in Splendeur Magazine's online blog.

Hilary is a sunrise chaser and adventure seeker. When she isn't finding a local coffee shop to frequent, she enjoys being surrounded by nature, traveling with her husband and their puppy, Aspen, listening to podcasts, and making memories with family and friends. Learn more about her at www.sweetteabythetree.com.